Critters

Books by A.B.C. Whipple

Yankee Whalers in the South Seas
Pirate: Rascals of the Spanish Main
Tall Ships and Great Captains
The Fatal Gift of Beauty:
The Final Years of Byron and Shelley
Vintage Nantucket
The Challenge
To the Shores of Tripoli:
The Birth of the U.S. Navy and Marines

With the Editors of Time-Life Books

Fighting Sail
The Whalers
The Clipper Ships
The Racing Yachts
The Mediterranean
Storm
Restless Oceans

For Young Readers

Famous Pirates of the New World
Hero of Trafalgar
The Mysterious Voyage of Captain Kidd

Critters

ADVENTURES IN WILDEST SUBURBIA

A.B.C. Whipple

Illustrations by John T. Burgoyne

ST. MARTIN'S PRESS
New York

The author wishes to thank *Reader's Digest* for permission to use the chapters on gulls, skunks, squirrels, and swans, shorter versions of which were originally written for that magazine.

The author also wishes to thank *Smithsonian* Magazine for permission to use the chapter on raccoons, which was originally written for that magazine.

In the chapter on gulls, the Ogden Nash poem is from *Verses from 1929 On* by Ogden Nash. Copyright 1940 by Ogden Nash. By permission of Little, Brown and Company.

Design by Sara Stemen

Library of Congress Cataloging-in-Publication Data

Whipple, A. B. C. (Addison Beecher Colvin)
    Critters : adventures in wildest suburbia / A.B.C. Whipple.
        p.   cm.
    "A Thomas Dunne Book".
    ISBN 0-312-10445-6 (hbk.)
    1. Urban fauna.   I. Title.
QH541.5.C6W48   1994
591.52'68—dc20   93-43902
                                                                CIP

A Thomas Dunne Book

First Edition: February 1994

10   9   8   7   6   5   4   3   2   1

Contents

Preface

Early last fall I witnessed an extraordinary sight: a couple of herring gulls actually feeding on herring. For generations the herring gulls in our neighborhood of Greenwich, Connecticut, have preferred the sandwiches of picnickers, the pizza crusts of the mall, and the garbage of the town dump. They have learned a simple lesson of life. Why go to all the trouble of diving into the water to catch fish when the nourishment of an effluent society is everywhere for the taking? For many years the only herring most of our herring gulls ever saw was in a discarded jar.

But something new has come to our town: recycling. The once-noisome landfill of trash and rotting garbage has been replaced by an enclosed building where waste is sorted into cans, bottles, paper, and food, all of which are sheltered from the gulls. Evidently as a result, some of our gulls have reverted to the feeding habits of their ancestors. So I watched in surprise as a flock of herring gulls, hovering and diving like terns, fished for their food.

It's an instructive little lesson in survival. My suburban neighbors use the town dump until it becomes intolerable and then switch to recycling. The herring gull, unable to alter things, simply adapts to the new food source. And

when it disappears, the gull reverts atavistically to the feeding habits of many generations earlier. Man disposes. The
gull adapts. Charles Darwin would have been amused.

We have seen little evidence, however, of any other
local bird or animal returning to its wild state. Skunks still
prefer our cellars and garages to den up for the winter.
Swans continue to opt for hand-tossed bread instead of
beach grass. Raccoons raid the garbage pails. Rabbits and
deer, making their prandial rounds of the neighborhood,
enjoy a wide selection, choosing from Mrs. Caulkins's carrots, Mrs. Pilert's lettuce, and Mrs. Baker's rutabagas, with
Mrs. Whipple's chives for seasoning. Squirrels outwit most
of our so-called squirrel-proof bird feeders. Canada geese
crop (and crap on) our lawns. Bats swoop in and out of
our attics. And mockingbirds perch on our TV antennas,
ceaselessly serenading them all. The artifacts of suburbanization—not the forests of their wild beginnings—are what
our critters like most.

It wasn't supposed to happen that way. When Americans first started moving out of the cities and into the
suburbs, it was naturally assumed that they would displace
the native fauna, driving them into the remaining forests.
Suburbanization started as early as the mid-nineteenth century, as soon as trains and trolleys provided the first efficient transportation for commuters. But it didn't reach
landslide proportions until the latter half of this century,
when workers fled the cities, to be followed shortly by
many of their employers as well. The 1990 U.S. Census
made it official. More Americans—some 115 million of
them—now live in the suburbs than in the cities or the
rural areas. And because the change, rapid as it has been in
recent years, has been going on for a century and a half,
many of the animals have had time to adapt.

Adapt they have, skillfully, shrewdly, and, one might

say, almost gleefully. Although there has been no official census of wildlife population in the United States, any homeowner can tell you that there has been a veritable population explosion in the suburbs of the very critters that were supposed to be endangered by human encroachment. Indeed, one animal expert calculates that many species "are in a better position than they have been in for perhaps three hundred years."

Not every species, of course. Many of the larger, wilder beasts—the bear, the moose, the coyote—have been driven away as their forest habitats were leveled. But even some of those animals seem to be making a tentative comeback. Bears, like gulls, have discovered the convenience of the dump. New Jersey, where only ten black bears were sighted as recently as 1976, now has an estimated 350; consequently, the state has had to set up two "emergency bear response" teams. A New Jersey animal expert reported, "It seems like every year there's less and less damage reports from farmers and more complaints from the suburbs." One bear even attempted to crash a West Milford wedding reception. In Connecticut a bear was seen paddling about in a Fairfield County swimming pool; bear sightings in this populous state nearly tripled between 1990 and 1991. One bear visited the suburb of West Hartford in a neighborhood so built up that a policeman firing at it instead shot out a home air conditioner.

Moose have appeared in New York State for the first time since the Civil War. At last count, Maine had some twenty thousand of them. A few years ago a bull moose entertained a Maine neighborhood when he mistook a domestic cow for a possible mate and devoted nearly a month to a frustrating courtship.

Coyotes seem to be making the strongest comeback, mainly in pursuit of the proliferating deer. They have also discovered suburban gardens and have been seen helping themselves to the local vegetables, washing them down with water from the nearest swimming pool. The phenomenon of the returning coyote may be another of nature's balancing acts. A major reason for the population explosion of most suburban wildlife is the lack of larger predators, driven out by the destruction of their forests. Now some are being lured back by the overabundance of this tempting food source.

Indeed, the U.S. population of whitetail deer has increased exponentially, some say pestilentially. There are an estimated 13 million of them today, probably more than when the *Mayflower* landed. (Not very good records were kept in the seventeenth century.) Most of the deer are in suburbia. Fairfield County, nearest to New York City, has more of them than any of Connecticut's rural counties. And not just deer. Our state's swan population has doubled. Westchester County has more raccoons than there were in the entire state of New York two centuries ago.

American suburbanites have encouraged this population explosion not only by replacing the forest with open fields and nourishing gardens, but also by hand-feeding the animals and birds. Ospreys returning to New England shoreside towns have been encouraged by special platforms erected for their lofty nests. Many homeowners have joined a project called the Backyard Wildlife Program, converting their lawns into animal habitats. One yard owned by Derr and Peggy Andrlik in Elgin, Illinois, for example, at last count sheltered one hundred ducks and an assortment of squirrels, foxes, woodchucks, and deer, not to mention two pyrrhuloxias that somehow traveled to Illinois from their native home in Mexico.

Responding to the lure of the suburbs, migrating birds have stopped migrating. Waterfowl that used to pass through on the flyway are now "short-stopping," as ornithologists describe it, when they find they can subsist comfortably on the suburbanites' bird feeders and bread crumbs. The population of ducks and geese in Connecticut has increased by 80 percent in recent years. And the bird feeders have also attracted predators that were once driven away. Snakes, owls, and hawks have returned to feed on the birds feeding at the feeders. One red-tailed hawk also picked off a couple of invading squirrels. Ornithologist Greg Butcher reported in 1991, "Five years ago it was rare to see a raptor at a feeder. Now they are regular visitors."

The most obvious, not to say obnoxious, example of short-stopping is the Canada goose, which has discovered the attractions of the golf courses and town parks and has settled in as a permanent resident. More and more southern birds have migrated north and remained there when they found the thousands of household bird feeders. The cardinal and the mockingbird are everywhere. Human handouts have also encouraged other birds to expand their territories. The red-tinged house wren spread north from Long Island, New York, to Maine and south to the Carolinas, increasing its population by several thousand percent. Wild turkeys have appeared in our town; one found the living easier when it joined a domestic flock.

A California suburb has had an infestation of some 150 peacocks, descendants of a pair that escaped into the wild from someone's estate; they are now enjoying the pansies and petunias of the town's gardens, meanwhile irritating the townspeople with their strident shrieks; one of them has a habit of perching on a roof and screeching down the chimney.

Even the butterfly has been fostered by suburbia. Florida's iridescent blue atala, considered nearly extinct in the 1960s after developers cut down its principal food, the palmlike coontie tree, has adapted by changing its diet to the sago palms that the new homeowners have planted for decoration. Atalas now flutter throughout the state.

Many once-wild critters have not only joined the suburbanites, but have also invaded their homes. When one of our neighbors installed a cat door, her cats disdained it (or couldn't figure out how to use it), but the local raccoons promptly discovered it and had to be shooed out. Not only the raccoons. One day she turned on her clothes dryer and was astonished by howls from within. She opened the door to find a bedraggled opossum, which her husband lured into a box and released a few miles away. Only a couple of months later she found her two young daughters cornering a skunk in the downstairs toilet. Exterminators were called, and the retaliating skunk's odor lingered in the house for weeks. This time the cat door was permanently closed.

Some brave, if not foolhardy, suburbanites go out to the dump to watch the feeding bears and even encourage their children to hand them marshmallows for dessert. A few homeowners go so far as to make pets of the local fauna. A Greenwich family pampered a young deer with a room of its own and a diet of dog biscuits and baby formula, until it grew too large and was released to an uncertain future in the woods.

Critters are also fostered by laws and regulations. Most suburban deer are protected from their human predators by understandable anti-hunting laws in settled neighborhoods. Environmentalists have also made their contribution. The ban on DDT has helped reverse the population decline of most birds. The Endangered Species Act has saved countless animals. The Florida alligator, once on the brink of extinction, has made such an impressive comeback that it has been removed from the endangered species list in eleven southeastern states. An alligator recently lunched on a snorkeler in Tallahassee. Florida's animal-control officers currently receive more than ten thousand calls per year from people pleading for the removal of alligators from golf courses, swimming pools, and condo lawns, in this case raising the question of who is invading whose turf.

Many birds threatened with extinction have made a dramatic comeback, not always to the benefit of their human neighbors. The laughing gull almost disappeared in the New York area until a wildlife area was established—unfortunately near Kennedy International Airport—whereupon the gulls prospered to the point of endangering humans (not to mention themselves) by flying into the airplanes. The brown pelican, another threatened species, has thrived under protection. A few have been sighted as far north as Long Island, New York. One of them brought down a $149 million B-1B bomber that had been designed as a flying "war room" to protect government leaders from a nuclear bomb strike.

Comes the paradox. Many of the same suburbanites who themselves have done the most to make the wild critters feel at home nevertheless complain bitterly about a phenomenon for which they have only themselves to blame. We protest when squirrels descend on our bird feeders, forgetting that they like to eat too. We leave our garbage out in cans, then grouse when the raccoons make a mess of it, as though we were expecting them to tidy up. We try to shoo Canada geese from the lawn, but insist on cutting it to the height they prefer.

In short, the wild critters have proved far more adaptable to us than we have to them. The scientists have a word for it; the birds and animals have become *anthropogenic*, meaning that they have adopted human characteristics. Meanwhile, we are supporting a flourishing business in critter control. Some forty "nuisance wildlife control operators" in Connecticut are employed by the state solely to remove furry and feathered intruders from residents' homes. In Greenwich alone, the Animal Control Office gets nearly sixty calls a year complaining about raccoons, fifty calls about deer, twenty about skunks, and twenty-five about other critters. The Bloomfield, New Jersey, neighborhood supports a private firm of "wildlife removal specialists" who charge as much as $150 per call. One of them marveled at his customers. "It's amazing," he said. "They come out here to get into the country, and the first thing they do is call us to get rid of the wildlife."

I have been observing these animals for some forty years in a sample habitat of about an acre alongside Greenwich Cove. For a few years I reacted to the occasional invasion like many of my neighbors. And like many of them, I was outwitted by the raccoon and rabbit, squirrel and skunk. My only defense, I realized, was to become an amateur critter-watcher, meanwhile reading about them and questioning zoologists on the subject. I soon concluded that the best rule of suburban coexistence was the old principle of "live and let live." So my initial reaction of angry frustration has given way to one of appreciation and even respect.

It may not be remarkable for animals to adjust to a changing food supply, overpopulation, or new predators. But mankind is potentially, if often heedlessly, the worst predator of all. By our criteria we are at the top of the evolutionary ladder, the first species with the ability to alter the balance of nature, but from the animals' point of view (if they have one) we must be the greatest scourge ever, defiling, defoliating, and destroying much of the planet we share with them. In fact, environmentalists, who most definitely do have a point of view, estimate that the present extinction rate for mammals on this earth is one thousand times greater than the rate during the late Pleistocene period, when nature took its course. How can an ordinary, garden-variety critter adapt to *that*?

Yet they have, at least those with whom I have become acquainted during the last few decades. So I have concluded that it is not asking too much to try to adapt to them. Now I lock up my garbage, keep my cellar windows closed, settle for the shrubs and plants the deer dislike, grow extra vegetables for the rabbits, and feed the squirrels as well as the birds. And I'm content to enjoy the soar of the gull, the dive of the bat, the scamper of the squirrel, the amble of the skunk, the glide of the swan, the bound of the deer, and the waddle of the raccoon. To paraphrase the well-known homily, if I can't lick 'em, I'll enjoy 'em.

A Skunk in the Cellar

W E met at the foot of the stairs. That is to say, he paused in his stroll long enough to fix me with a beady eye of disdain before waddling on to his destination—which I did not stop to find out. There are eleven steps down into our cellar, and I touched about three of them on my way up-stairs to report to my wife that there was a skunk in the basement.

"You don't have to shout," she said. Clearly she did not appreciate the gravity of the situation.

In panic I called the local ASPCA. Yes, replied the young woman who answered the phone, skunks do get into cellars in the fall. "They are, like, looking for a real warm place, okay?" As she talked, or tried to, I recalled that the previous week I had opened two cellar windows to air out the place after a stuffy summer. No, the ASPCA did not remove skunks from people's houses, the girl explained. "You might, you know, put a plank up to a cellar window so he can, like, climb out, okay?"

After another peek into the cellar to make sure it had not been a hallucination, I changed into my oldest clothes, breathed a silent prayer, gingerly carried a long plank down the steps, opened the window farthest from the skunk, placed the plank in position, and perched on the topmost step to watch.

Evidently intrigued, the skunk walked a short way up the plank and surveyed the view. A cold late-October wind gusted through the open window and a few snowflakes flurried past. The skunk backed off the plank and sauntered away, shaking his head. (I say "his," though I did not know the skunk's sex and had no intention of trying to find out.) Thinking that perhaps the skunk might reconsider, I left the plank in place with the window open—until, a few hours later, realizing with horror that I was inviting a whole herd of skunks into the cellar, I closed the window (from the outside).

My next move was to the local library, on the principle of Know Thine Enemy. Collecting half a dozen books (and wondering why most of them were in the juvenile department), I sat down to study the American skunk.

There are, I found, nearly a dozen species within three genera, or groups: the rare, randomly striped spotted skunk, the snout-muzzled hog-nosed skunk of Central and South America, and the best-known (if hardly best-loved) striped skunk. The latter inhabits North America from Hudson Bay to northern Mexico and from coast to coast. In the U.S. suburbs where we humans have provided a more appealing habitat than the forest—especially houses with warm cellars—the striped skunk has adapted quite well. Zoologists estimate that its population is probably at an all-time high. Thus the most likely species to turn up in your cellar or mine is the striped skunk *(Mephitis mephitis)*.

Mephitis is Latin for "noxious exhalation"—i.e., stink. So *Mephitis mephitis* obviously means stink times two. The common name "skunk" comes from the Algon-quian *segonku*. French Canadians had an apt name for it: *enfant du diable*, child of the devil. In various parts of the United States the skunk has other nicknames (some unprintable) including "wood pussy" and "polecat"; actually, the true polecat *(Mustela putorius)* is our skunk's European cousin. But the skunk is not a member of the cat family. It is a mustelid, related to badgers, weasels, martins, and otters. Many mustelids employ a bad-smelling musk to mark their territory or ward off attackers. But this notorious defense mechanism reaches its supreme development in the skunk. It consists of two glands located under the tail, capable of blasting the wondrously effective musk accurately for up to ten feet. (The exact range seems not to have been measured; I'm not surprised.)

Though other animals are equipped with tooth and/ or claw, the skunk requires no such armament. (It does, however, have sharp digging claws.) And though most nocturnal animals' backs are darker than their bellies to provide camouflage at night, the skunk's coloration is exactly opposite: the white blaze on its nose and the white stripe along its back clearly advertise that this is a critter not to be messed with.

Mammalogists call this "aposematic coloration"; the skunk shares it with only a few other animals, including the American porcupine, whose sharp quills are white-tipped. Aposematic-colored animals generally have small ears, are nearsighted, and move slowly (though in an emergency a skunk can lope at up to ten miles an hour), since they have little need for warning of predators. It is the predator who has to watch out.

The skunk's powerful defense has an understandable effect on its personality. Your average animal relies on stealth and flees from danger. The skunk proceeds on its lordly way with near-total disregard for attackers. One naturalist reported on a skunk facing down a six-foot, 350-pound bear that evidently had had some previous experience; another recalled watching five bears being driven from their dinner by the appearance of one skunk. Dogs and cats, usually after one encounter with a skunk, readily surrender their dinner bowls.

Evidently the skunk has only two effective enemies: the great horned owl, which is capable of swooping down and snatching it aloft before it can retaliate, and the automobile. Accustomed to being shunned by all, the skunk expects an oncoming car to do likewise, with dire results for both skunk and car. There was a time when the hunter and trapper were among the skunk's deadliest predators; furriers paid well for skunk pelts, which they euphemistically labeled "Alaskan sable" or "black martin." But an honest-labeling law put an end to that business, since there was little market for skunk fur. So a modern skunk that escapes both owl and automobile can expect to live about eight to ten years.

Some experts maintain that a skunk will almost never fire its deadly weapon if it is treated with kindness. In *Thistle & Co.*, a memoir of her experience with various adopted wild animals, Era Zistel described a skunk she rescued and nursed back to health. It submitted to pills forced down its throat, adapted to hissing, roughhousing cats, and enjoyed sleeping in its benefactor's bed while crooning her to sleep. It also terrified the neighbors by chasing them in hopes of being picked up.

But her cuddly pet bore no resemblance to my visitor, who obviously regarded me as an intruder in my cellar. On my nervous visits to the top of the stairs, I usually found him curled up in a corner; invariably he would open one sleepy eye for a moment, close it with a sigh of resignation, and resume his interrupted nap.

This skunk, I was convinced, was quite prepared to shoot first and ask no questions later. And think of what a skunk could do to an enclosed cellar, I thought. We would probably have to move out. How much could you get for a house reeking with skunk smell? In fact, we had been planning to go away on a sabbatical for three months starting in January, a project that required renting out the house. How do you rent a house with a skunk in the cellar? Not only did I have to get that animal out of there; I also had a deadline.

Since he could not be forcibly evicted, the only alternative was to outsmart him. So I concentrated on my study of *Mephitis mephitis*, while my wife commented on the ludicrous contrast of the skunk contentedly basking below while I anxiously prepared for what she clearly regarded as an uneven contest of wits.

Reading on, I found that the American striped skunk inhabits all the continental United States. A solitary, self-sufficient, mostly nocturnal mammal, it is territorial and uses small amounts of its scent to mark its boundaries. It feeds on insects, grasshoppers, snakes, turtles, berries, and eggs of ground-nesting birds. It cannot climb trees. Often a skunk can be seen nosing along a highway, looking for road kills. Skunks sometimes compete with raccoons at suburban garbage cans. Evidently they are immune to the sting of a bee; there have been reports of skunks tapping beehives and gobbling up the inhabitants as they swarmed out to investigate. Frequently the skunk is blamed for killing chickens, but apparently this is a bum rap. A U.S. Department of Agriculture study examined the stomachs of 1,700 skunks and found plenty of eaten insects, fruit, grains, and tiny animals, but no chicken remains. Chicken kills are usually the work of the skunk's cousins, the weasel and mink. In fact, the skunk is sometimes known as "the farmer's friend" because it consumes so many marauding insects.

By the onset of winter in colder climates, the skunk has put on a layer of fat and is searching for a warm refuge like my cellar. The skunk does not actually hibernate; instead it sleeps through the coldest weather and ventures out only on mild days for a midwinter snack.

By spring it is on the prowl again. And although it has lost as much as half of its body weight, its chief immediate interest is in mating. The male is the more active of the species, going from one female's den to another until he is invited in. Occasionally there is a battle between two males for the favors of a female, resulting in a stench that radiates for miles.

Not only is he an unsavory lover, but shortly after mating the skunk walks out on his pregnant partner, leaving her to deliver the young about nine weeks later, a litter of four to six kits, which she raises as a single parent. I recalled that a few years earlier a neighbor had had a mother skunk deliver three babies in his cellar, and I prayed that mine was indeed a "he."

Within three weeks the young have opened their eyes and have grown their distinctive, glossy black-and-white fur. Three weeks later the mother takes them foraging. Unlike most young mammals, which bumble off in all directions, the nearsighted baby skunks follow their mother in a straight line, each with its nose under the tail of its brother or sister. If one strays, it quickly loses sight of its family and screams until its mother noses it back into line. During this period the mother is a fierce defender of her young, which may explain the frequency of skunk smells in our neighborhood in early summer. Within a couple of months the young skunks are ready to strike out on their own.

Already the young skunk has developed its powerful musk glands. When threatened—ah, here was what I

needed to know—the skunk reacts with a sharp hiss, stamping its feet and lifting its tail as further warning. If the intruder does not back off (as most animals do, either from instinct or memorable experience), the skunk twists its body into a U-shape so it can take aim. This is its final notice, after which the skunk contracts the muscles activating the two nozzles protruding under its tail to let fly twin jets of an oily, acid, yellowish liquid that quickly turns into a noisome mist engulfing everyone and everything within about ten feet.

The skunk aims for the enemy's eyes, which the mist temporarily blinds; it also sticks to the victim's skin, burning it and covering it with a vile-smelling odor that can last for days. (The skunk's protruding glands protect it from the same effect.) Although this first blast is the strongest, the skunk is capable of letting go half a dozen before having to wait for its glands to store up more ammunition. There are those who claim that you can escape the spray by sneaking up on the skunk from the rear and lifting it by the tail so it cannot fire. I don't recommend it. The skunk is nearsighted, but it can sense an attacker's presence. And what if you make the grab and miss?

Few odors are as persistent as that of a skunk's emission. Frequently a spraying on our lawn has been strong enough to wake me in the middle of the night. Various antidotes have been proferred to remove the smell from one's clothes or, more likely, from the blundering family dog: stale beer, tomato juice, vinegar, bleach, gasoline, ammonia, even douche. One friend claims that a well-known brand of shampoo turned her dog from a pariah to an attraction just in time for a wedding party. But usually only time will gradually erase the lingering smell.

Skunk musk, chemically called butylmercapton, is unsurpassed in the laboratory. Tiny amounts of it are mixed with expensive perfumes to preserve the odor of the perfume. Utility companies also use skunk musk in their pipelines to signal a gas leak.

The books were helpful in telling me what not to do, but they weren't a great deal of help in getting rid of my cellar-dwelling nemesis. I found myself spending most of my weekends at the top of the stairs, contemplating what ruse could be employed to lure the animal outdoors, to the ill-concealed disgust of my wife, who seemed to think there were more important things to do around the house.

The books also told me that skunks were not noted for their brainpower, since they had little need for it. I was inclined to doubt this claim, having also read about those bees and about skunks that had kicked eggs along the ground to break them, and others that had rolled woolly caterpillars in the dust to brush off their bristly hair. A neighbor told me about a skunk that burrowed under his garage. Hearing that skunks hated the smell of mothballs, he tossed some down the hole, only to have the skunk toss them right back.

But another neighbor with considerable skunk experience told me that they loved tuna fish. Here was a chance to prove the natural superiority of human intelligence. Checking to make sure that my skunk was at a safe distance, I carefully deposited a dollop of tuna on each step of the cellar stairs, plus a trail out through the cellar door. My wife, who was finally getting into the spirit of the thing, spread a thin layer of flour near the door. Now all I had to do was wait until I saw skunk tracks in the flour. I settled down to watch a football game on TV while my ingenious plan did its work.

At the end of the first quarter I peered out the window. Already there were tiny tracks in the flour. I bolted out and slammed the cellar door—thereby closing the trap on a local cat that was finishing the last of the tuna. With the bait gone, the cat was glad to get out. The skunk meanwhile slept through the entire performance.

The next move, it turned out, was the skunk's. He disappeared.

Because the cellar leaks in rainy weather, we do not use it for storage, so there was no place for him to hide. But he was nowhere in sight. The cellar windows and door had been closed since my two abortive experiments. How had he gotten out?

The American striped skunk, the books said, is about the size of a house cat. But because so much of the skunk is fur, it can squeeze through seemingly impassable holes. Apparently he had found a tiny escape hatch hitherto unknown to me.

Now I had a new worry. Could he come and go at will? For the next week I checked the cellar every evening when I came home from work. No sign of him. Apparently he had concluded that he would never get his winter's sleep with all my interruptions, and had gone looking for a quieter den.

If so, his decision was well timed, since we had found a potential tenant. After showing him around the house, I led him to the cellar to see the furnace, chuckling as I recounted my recent adventure. "Last month a skunk got into the cellar, but we got rid of him—MIGAWD, THERE HE IS AGAIN!" As my would-be tenant beat a retreat, the skunk plodded contentedly across the floor, pausing only long enough to view us with haughty disdain.

The skunk visitation had become a major skunk mystery. Not only was he appearing and disappearing as if by magic, but now the distinctive white stripe on his back had become a blue-white scar. What on earth was going on?

My vigil time at the top of the stairs increased. For the next few days I assumed the lookout position every morning and evening, watching for the animal and trying to figure out his escape route. Finally the mystery solved itself.

The skunk had disappeared again. But as I rose to give up for the day, there was a sharp click from the gas water heater, followed by a quick scurrying sound as the skunk shot out through the water-heater door. While the heater's gas ignited, the skunk ambled over to the sump pump for a drink and settled down to continue his nap.

Skunks, I had read, not only like warm, dark places to den up for the winter; the warmer the spot, the better they like it. Our intruder had discovered the warmth of the water heater and had climbed in to bask under the pilot light, secure from the nuisance of my constant intrusions. Obviously he had soon discovered the danger of his hiding place: the igniting heater had burned the white hair off his back as he fled. But he had quickly learned how to escape in the fraction of a second between the click of the heater's thermostat and the ignition of the burner. So while I had been searching the corners of the cellar, he had been curled up out of sight, often within a foot of me as I walked by his refuge.

Desperate measures were called for. I turned to our son, who, with the incurable optimism of a teenager, enlisted a brave, foolhardy young friend for the challenge. Opening the cellar window, raising the plank again, and arming themselves with pans, hockey sticks, and cans of moth spray, the two boys advanced relentlessly and noisily on the skunk. Hearing the din from below, my wife muttered, "Oh dear, not in his school clothes!" and began collecting cans of tomato juice.

"The books say that stale beer is best for washing out skunk smell," I informed her.

"If we wait for you to let a beer go stale," she replied, "the skunk will be a grandfather. I'll stick to tomato juice."

I returned to the top of the stairs. The skunk was studying the boys with a puzzled expression. He looked up at the open window and back again at the outlandish noisemakers. He did not hiss a warning, stamp his feet or turn in the typical U shape to fire his spray. Instead he slowly ambled up the plank and out the window, which the boys slammed shut with shouts of triumph. Through the window I watched the skunk walk away, shaking his head in what looked like pure disgust.

A few days later we had a blizzard. Watching the

slashing clouds of snow, I was suddenly filled with re-
morse. Had I driven my skunk out to perish in the storm?
Had he found another warm den? Was a more hospitable
soul sheltering him from the frigid temperatures? With no
white stripe on his back, would he become prey to some
predator because he could not flaunt his defense? Or had
he slowly frozen to death, an innocent victim of my
selfishness?

We had to wait until spring for the answer. A few days
after we had returned from my sabbatical, our son's friend
dropped by. "Guess who I saw in the park yesterday?" he
asked. Attracted by a scuffling noise in an overturned trash
can late one afternoon, he had watched as a skunk emerged
amid the fast-food remnants. The blue-black scar down
the animal's back was unmistakable as the skunk waddled
contentedly off to the next trashcan to resume his supper.

He hasn't come back to our house; obviously he has
had enough of us. Now our visiting skunk is a handsome
creature with an extraordinarily broad white stripe (perhaps
an even more blatant warning). In fact, there seems to be
a family of them. We've seen two or three together, just at
dusk, nosing across the lawn and digging for grubs. My
initial annoyance at having to replace their divots gave way
to approbation when I read that they were eating Japanese
beetle larvae. The local birds approve, too. The next day
they flock to feed on the overturned soil. And I've convinced myself that it is good for the grass.

Meanwhile there are cobwebs on our cellar windows.
They haven't been opened since.

TWO

Raccoons in the Garbage

Of all the wild critters that inhabit—or infest—our neighborhood, the one that has made itself most at home is the raccoon. Alternately loved and hated, regarded as cute and cuddly or a masked bandit, the raccoon waddles around Greenwich, delighting our children, dining on our garbage, pushing in and out of our cat doors, and evidently delighting in frustrating our dogs. Our neighborhood poet laureate, Pyke Johnson, summed it up neatly:

> The raccoon wears a mask at night
> And has a brown-ringed tail,
> Which is how I recognize him
> When he dumps my garbage pail.

And not just in our neighborhood, I find. According to the newspapers, so many raccoons invaded the outer fringes of Washington, D.C., that one Washingtonian captured a few and transported them to northern Virginia for what the columnist called "a new and better life among the nuts and berries," a characterization that did not amuse some Virginians. Meanwhile, suburban Virginians were

13

trapping their raccoons and releasing *them* in Washington's Rock Creek Park.

In a Boston suburb, a lady who had ordered cookies by mail discovered a ripped-open box on her porch, a few crumbs and a well-fed raccoon shuffling down the steps.

Other suburbanites, foolish enough to leave food on their patios for a few minutes, frequently share the food with raccoons; one of them deftly lifted the lid of a barbecue and made off with a steak awaiting the fire.

In my own attempts to cope with our raccoon invasion, I once again turned to what my wife called "defensive reading." Among other studies of the subject, I encountered a sober-sided monograph titled *The Ecology of Urban Raccoons in Cincinnati, Ohio*, published in 1974, in which two University of Cincinnati biologists, James R. Schinner and Darrell L. Cauley, reported on twenty-seven months spent prowling the Cincinnati suburb of Clifton. Their conclusions, "after a total of 3,452 trap nights," were that the suburb was "ideally suited for maximal raccoon activity," and that "garbage is an important food source."

I could have told them that. A second such report on suburban wildlife, done by Mr. Cauley in Taylor, Michigan, a suburb of Detroit, also confirmed my own observations. "Four hundred seventy-eight trap nights were recorded for raccoons," Mr. Cauley reported, "with a total of nine captures, for a capture frequency of 1.9 percent." In other words, most of the raccoons were too smart for the traps.

Indeed, it has been my experience that in the contest between the wily raccoon invader and its wary human host, the former has usually demonstrated a quite superior intelligence. The species *Procyon lotor*, in Greenwich anyway, has outwitted, baffled, frustrated, and enraged *Homo sapi-*

ens often enough to make one question the translation of *sapiens*.

Both scientific studies prove that there are a lot of raccoons in the suburbs; in Clifton there were as many as one per 1.4 acres, a high population density, to borrow the phrase. And they do get around. A Taylor raccoon covered a sixty-four-acre feeding area.

I could have told the biologists that, too. For some years I have been conducting, mostly involuntarily, my own unscientific study of *Procyon lotor*. The central site of my study has been a garbage can in a well with pedal-operated lid, located at our back door. For more than twenty years it foiled every dog and other scavenger in the community. Until recently it was also too much for the raccoons.

It could, I suppose, be another example of evolution in action, the wild critter adapting to a suburban challenge. For whatever reason, our evening quiet was increasingly broken by a clanging of the garbage-can lid. Inspecting the site one night, I found the lid closed, but I could hear unmistakable shuffling noises within the recesses of the garbage can. As I approached it, the top opened, lifted by the head of a large raccoon, which nimbly climbed out, glanced my way with what I took to be a look of gratitude, and sauntered away.

In hindsight, I realize that it was a look of benign contempt. Evidently our garbage was not up to the standards of the habitat, because on subsequent nights our visitor took to hauling the plastic bags from the can and distributing the contents about the driveway, evidently to sort the tasty from the inedible. Studying the detritus, I almost concluded that the raccoon was laying out the courses of its dinner; one morning I found a spread of shrimp shells, followed by clean-picked chicken bones, followed by cheese and crackers, followed by a cigar butt.

To defend our garbage from these nocturnal depradations, I engaged in a battle of wits with my visitor. I should have known better. Heavy rocks atop the garbage-can lid, moth flakes, sprays, "raccoon-proof" clamps—all met their match. As I write, the battle appears to have reached a stalemate. A hinge on one side of the can, a hasp and clip on the other, and a spring lock across the can top seem to have defeated the raccoons—but, I'm sure, only temporarily. It may also help that the garbage and trash cans are now inside the garage. But with fingers bandaged from cuts incurred while drilling the hinge holes, with insomnia from listening through the night for further incursions, and with a numbing realization that I have met my match, I await the night they learn how to open the garage door and snap that spring lock.

The experience, added to my reading, has taught me a great deal about *Procyon lotor* in its suburban habitat. The most casual observation dispels one or two of the most widely accepted raccoon myths. The raccoon does not, for example, have that marvel of evolution, the opposable thumb—not yet, anyway. But it has so perfected its ability to grasp with its two outside claws that the result is nearly the same. A raccoon lifting the top of a trash can exactly resembles a human lifting a pot lid. A raccoon sifting through its dinner with its handlike paws would shame a child.

But, to dispel another myth, the raccoon is far from the dainty, hygienic creature of legend, delicately washing its food and cleaning up its debris. A selective feeder it is; neat it is not. So widely accepted is the notion of the hygienic raccoon that part of its name, *lotor*, is Latin for "washer." (*Procyon* is the Greek name for a double star that rises before Sirius, the dog star, and was given to the raccoon when it was discovered not to be a dog, as had previously been assumed; in fact, the raccoon is more closely related to the panda.) The assumption of daintiness came from the raccoon's habit of dipping its food in water when water is available. The raccoon does not do this to clean its food; indeed, it frequently urinates in the same water.

In all my reading I could find no convincing explanation of the raccoon's "washing" behavior. The most likely suggestion is that it is a hangover from the raccoon's earliest hunting methods, which consisted of feeling along the bottom of a stream for crayfish and similar prey. Given the opportunity, and a lack of convenient garbage, the raccoon still gropes underwater for food. In the process it does not look at what it is doing, but evidently watches out for danger.

If daintiness is not one of the raccoon's attributes, gluttony is. The raccoon is omnivorous, readily eating berries and baby birds, corn and crayfish, moles, voles, and garbage. I doubt that even a teenage boy's appetite matches that of a raccoon. But with intelligence superior to most teenage boys, the raccoon suits its feeding to the season, preferring protein-rich foods during the spring and summer, when it is most active, and carbohydrates in the autumn, when it is storing up fat for its winter sleep.

The raccoon does not, however, hibernate like such animals as the bat and the opossum, both of whose temperatures drop and metabolisms slow throughout the winter. In northern latitudes the raccoon retires to its den for most of the winter; wisely, it hates to walk in the snow. Its hideaway is usually a hollow in a tree, but it can also be a small cave. During the winter the raccoon sleeps for days or weeks, but awakens to forage again when the temperature rises above twenty-eight degrees Fahrenheit. Our garbage collector was as sorry as I to hear that.

By spring the raccoon is lean and hungry, having lost nearly half its weight. But it shortly remedies this situation. By early summer a full-grown raccoon is nearly three feet long and weighs about fifteen pounds. By autumn, through the largesse of its human neighbors, it eats as much as four pounds of food every night, and nearly doubles its weight. One that may be a record size weighed in at sixty-two pounds; it was four feet seven inches long from nose to tail tip. The largest raccoon in our habitat more nearly resembles P. G. Wodehouse's famous sow, the Empress of Blandings.

Once it is full-grown, the raccoon fears few predators. I wondered why the many dogs in our neighborhood did not help thin the raccoon population, if only by occasionally stumbling onto one. But I realized why when one night *I* stumbled into the path of a young raccoon and was attacked by its snarling, fang-baring mother.

For a raccoon to outwit and outbluff the singularly inept dogs of our area is not surprising. But raccoon lore includes many accounts of the animal's superior intelligence. The most highly trained hounds have been baffled by raccoons that doubled and redoubled their tracks, ran along the tops of fences, climbed trees, leaped from one tree to another, and plunged into streams to lose their scent. Despite its waddling gait, the raccoon can reach a top speed of fifteen miles an hour in short bursts. It can also lure a dog to its death. Plunging into a lake or cove, it swims out into deep water. When the dog swims after it, the raccoon circles the struggling pursuer, climbs onto its neck, and holds its head under until the dog drowns.

The raccoon's intelligence is nearly matched by its strength and ferocity. One raccoon with a good foothold in its tree suspended in midair a two-hundred-pound Yale professor who had grabbed it by the tail. A cornered raccoon backs up against a wall, rock, or tree trunk to avoid being attacked from behind; and with its slashing claws and needle-sharp teeth it can disembowel or cut the jugulars of two or three dogs its size or larger.

When not on the defensive, the raccoon is normally a friendly, if messy, critter. Another sign of its intelligence is its highly developed curiosity, which, combined with its efficient claws, can make it an extremely annoying neighbor. Raccoons have been known to lift a door latch, walk into a kitchen, open the refrigerator, and help themselves. Raccoons can turn doorknobs and pry open windows. They are also quick to spot and take advantage of cat doors.

A friend of mine, still half asleep one morning, was rudely awakened when he opened a kitchen cupboard door and stared into the face of a raccoon; a few days earlier his son had chased three of them out through the cat door. A suburbanite who fancied expensive tropical fish found the aquarium empty one day and spotted a raccoon ambling away from the door it had pushed open. Raccoons can also turn on faucets (which they rarely bother to turn off), unscrew bottle tops, and pull corks; on occasion, a raccoon stumbling home in the early morning hours like a drunk is just that.

The raccoon not only pays visits on suburbanites; it can also move right in. One of its favorite nesting sites is a chimney, especially when the damper is closed. Since the raccoon marks its territory with urine, its presence in the chimney shortly becomes noticeable, not to say noisome. Some raccoons are adept enough to raise the damper and explore—i.e., make an unholy mess of—the rooms below. Fleas and ticks also tend to leave their raccoon hosts and invade the house.

But the most traumatic invasion I've heard of occurred when a friend opened her damper and lit a fire before her unknown visitor had climbed all the way up the chimney. She was suddenly confronted with a screaming, flaming raccoon, racing about the living room in a cloud of smoke, ashes, and soot.

Another neighbor was plagued by raccoons climbing up to the widow's walk on his roof. This would not have bothered him except that they seemed to be using it for a toilet, soiling the side of the house; perhaps raccoons are frightened by heights. A rare suburbanite smarter than the raccoon, he found that they were climbing a downspout and promptly coated it with Vaseline. After what he describes as a few comical attempts by his furry climbers, they gave up.

Attics also seem to appeal to raccoons, and once they have settled in, they are difficult to dislodge. One unwilling but ingenious host managed to drive off the invaders by blasting rock music into the attic. A neighbor resorted to exterminators who employed humane traps; he was amused to note that their most successful bait was a Big Mac. But another friend who attempted a more direct method—a .22 rifle—to drive a raccoon off his back porch now wishes he hadn't.

With rifle loaded and ready, my friend retired and was soon awakened from a fitful sleep by the noise of a falling garbage-can lid. Sneaking downstairs in his pajamas, he took up his trusty rifle, eased open the back door, and flipped on the light. Perched on the edge of the garbage can was a large raccoon, its eyes gleaming in the light. The gun went off, the raccoon jumped down, and my friend shot his Buick, shattering the windshield.

Like skunks, some raccoons prefer cellars for their winter dens, leading to an apocryphal story about the resident of a nearby town who telephoned the police department, was put through to the chief, and reported, "There's a coon in my cellar!"

The police chief, who happened to be black, reacted by chiding the caller for his language. "Sir, if there is a black man in your cellar, just say so. Please do not use words like 'coon.' "

There was a pause before the caller replied. "I don't understand. *I'm* black, and I've got this raccoon in my cellar . . ."

Farmers are not amused by their raccoon neighbors, since corn, milk, honey, and chickens are among the raccoon's favorite foods. In midsummer the raccoons move methodically and efficiently through a cornfield, opening the ears to see if they are ripe and having a feast if they are. One raccoon regularly milked a farmer's cow. A bird lover watched a mother raccoon climb out on a tree limb, suspend herself by her hind legs, and unhook a hanging bird feeder, sending it crashing to the ground in front of her waiting kits.

The raccoon's superior intellect sometimes tends to induce a sense of confidence bordering on bravado. A forest ranger claims to have seen a group of campers around a fire joined by raccoons that gradually edged closer to the circle, their beady eyes registering supplication, until they were sitting with their hosts, enjoying the firelight and munching hot dogs. At least the forest ranger did not claim that they joined in the singing.

They do give voice, usually in churring undertones and chirping calls. A raccoon can also hiss like a goose, growl like a dog, snarl like a tiger, or screech like an owl. A tame raccoon will, when stroked under the chin, purr like a cat. But when confronted with danger, a raccoon can emit a scream that would shame a banshee.

Raccoons are capable not only of mastering door latches, locks, and even zippers (some of which are beyond my capability), but have also done extremely well in psychologists' studies, in mazes and in multiple-choice tests. They learn quickly, have good memories, and their skill improves with age. Certainly, *Procyon lotor old greenwich* evidences many symptoms of intellect superior to that of *Homo sapiens old greenwich*. The male raccoon, for example, is openly polygamous; few of the male humans in our suburban ecosystem are so frank about it. In a behavior pattern perhaps similar to that of some of its human counterparts, the male raccoon sets out in early spring and prowls from den to den in search of a temporary mate. Occasionally, males will quarrel over a female in front of her den, but the female is the one who makes the choice. The pair thereupon den up for a week or two, after which the male, exhibiting signs of fatigue, goes on his way.

The female feeds voraciously during the first few weeks of her sixty-three-day pregnancy, then holes up in her den to give birth to two to seven kits. At birth they weigh about two ounces and are blind and helpless. Within three weeks, however, their eyes are open and their mother is taking them out for walks to learn about their habitat.

She devotes the next few weeks to teaching them how to grope for crayfish, crack birds' eggs, and, in our area, open garbage cans. The mother weans her kits by the time they are fourteen weeks old, no doubt because their sharp teeth are beginning to appear. The fatherless family generally stays together through the summer and autumn and sometimes into the winter, until the mother finally drives the children out on their own and prepares to examine the new season's suitors to select the father of her next family. Barring accident or disease, her kits will live about ten years.

She and her ancestors have been bringing up their families this way for more centuries than humans have. Raccoons, as my wife reminded me at the height of my angry frustration, were in the New World long before we were. Indeed, they exist only in the New World, and have been here for nearly 30 million years. Captain John Smith first mentioned the "Aroughcun" in his dispatches in 1612, and the early settlers were soon complaining about raccoons eating their corn. The settlers also found an intriguing use for this odd creature: its penis contains a bone that makes an excellent pipe cleaner.

Like everyone since, the settlers were impressed by

the raccoon's ingenuity and gumption, one observer even claiming to have seen a raccoon fishing for crabs with its tail. Another of man's reactions was characteristic: he started killing the raccoon. But its meat is too fatty to be very palatable. Its dense fur, however, provided excellent protection during the North American winters. The first raccoon coat of which I've read was worn by the Indian chief Powhatan as a mark of his eminence. It was adorned with raccoon tails, a design that unfortunately did not survive to the days of the coat's popularity on college campuses. The raccoon itself recognized the warming properties of its distinctive ringed tail long before the trappers did. When the raccoon lies up for a spell of winter, it curls itself into a ball, with its warm tail wrapped around most of its body, providing nature's finest insulation. Humans found the tail equally comfortable when left on a raccoon hat and wrapped around the neck. Some settlers in effect wore an entire raccoon, with its face in front and its tail dangling at the back of the wearer's neck. Raccoon hats are waterproof as well as warm.

Despite nineteenth-century trappers and twentieth-century flappers, the hardy raccoon has survived in all the continental states, evolving into at least nineteen species and subspecies ranging from diminutive three-pound creatures in the Florida Keys to thirty-pound monsters in Maine and Minnesota. (Texas, naturally, also claims to have outsized specimens.) There is even a "wetback" raccoon, *Procyon lotor mexicanus*, which swims across the Rio Grande into Texas. The famous naturalist Ernest Thompson Seton estimated that there were 5 million raccoons in North and South America when the first settlers arrived. The best guess is that there are about the same number now. Thus the raccoon, unlike man, appears to have achieved zero population growth.

But recently the raccoon has been faced with another major threat. A particular strain of rabies that seems to affect raccoons more than other animals has spread up the East Coast. A disoriented rabid raccoon can bite household pets that have not been vaccinated against rabies (though by law they must be), and saliva from an infected dog or cat can infect its owner. The treatment is less painful than in earlier years; it consists of five injections instead of the thirty or so once required. (And since the course of treatments costs about one thousand dollars, a vaccinated pet at eight dollars is obviously a better investment.)

Understandably, many suburbanites have panicked at the prospect of rabid raccoon attacks, and our town's police have responded according to the perhaps understandable principle that a raccoon behaving oddly may be rabid. Since there is no method for diagnosing raccoon rabies without killing the animal, the police have been shooting any suspicious raccoon. That seems to include raccoons wandering about in the daylight, since they are largely nocturnal, though in our area many of them have become so accustomed to people that they forage during the day if they are hungry enough.

It was about 5:00 P.M. one day last summer when a policeman knocked on our door. "I just wanted you to know we'll be shooting over your seawall," he said. "There's a raccoon out there in the mud."

It was the first I knew of the town's policy. "There's nothing wrong with that raccoon," I protested. "I see it regularly. It often goes clamming at low tide."

"He's out in daylight, and we have orders to shoot any raccoon out in daylight because it might be rabid. Not their regular behavior."

"But this one won't hurt anybody," I argued.

"He might bite a dog or a child. Sorry, I don't make

the rules." The policeman signaled to his companion in the squad car and they advanced, revolvers in hand, on the seawall.

The raccoon was plodding through the mud, stopping periodically to listen for the motion or squirt of a hidden clam. As it turned its head to listen, it caught sight of the cops and, with a burst of speed I would not have believed possible, shot up the seawall steps and off between the houses, with the police in hot pursuit.

I heard no gunfire; the policemen wisely refrained from firing their guns in among the houses, as the raccoon apparently knew they would. It escaped. The next day it was back at the tideline, clamming again—this time, it seemed to me, with a wary eye on the seawall.

Rabies may be another of nature's balances. Although I know of no official count, my neighbors and I agree that the local raccoon population went into decline with the arrival of rabies in 1991. But by mid-1993 the epidemic appeared to have run its course, perhaps because it had indeed lowered the population of the local fauna. Our town, which recorded twenty-six cases of rabies among the neighborhood wildlife in the first three months of 1992, had only one in the same period of 1993. Nearby Stamford had none. The disease meanwhile has been reported farther north and east in Connecticut, where presumably it will curb the wildlife population for a couple of years as it has in Greenwich. If indeed it is nature's plan, nature probably will have the assistance of the local police of those communities, as it has in lower Fairfield County.

Some suburbanites have, perhaps unwisely, attempted to protect the resident raccoons from rabies by capturing baby raccoons and trying to bring them up as protected, inoculated pets. Young raccoons can be taught all sorts of tricks and seem to enjoy the process. At maturity, however, which comes at about two years, raccoons make themselves so obnoxious that usually they have to be released. So long as they are free to come and go, raccoons will avail themselves of the advantages of human hospitality. One raccoon regularly called at its benefactor's back door and rang a dinner bell to announce its arrival. Another returned with a dozen friends; they formed a queue, each waiting its turn to be fed.

But modern raccoons, it appears, cannot live by bread alone. Most of them, for example, appreciate a good cigar; showing more sense than humans, they prefer rolling a stogie in their paws to' smoking it. One indulgent host claims to have been visited frequently by a raccoon that sits on his sofa watching television, yawning during commercials and on occasion switching channels. Another TV owner is visited by a raccoon that especially likes ballet. Raccoons do not care whether the television is color or black-and-white; they are color blind.

But the most convincing testimony I have heard to the natural intellectual superiority of the raccoon is sworn to by a music lover who claims that a neighborhood raccoon is a Beethoven fan. It prefers the Ninth Symphony. When the Ninth starts booming through the open windows, the raccoon promptly comes out of the woods, unlatches the screen door, walks to one of the speakers, and sits beside it, immobile and unblinking, until the last notes have sounded. Then it rises quietly, lets itself out, and returns to the forest.

That, I suppose, is worth a lot of garbage.

THREE

Squirrels in the Bird Feeder

In the beginning it was strictly for the birds. Beguiled by dozens of singing visitors, I bought a feeder and hung it from the nearest tree. Obviously it was an immediate success; I had to refill it twice a day. I was congratulating myself when my wife gently pointed out that our local birds could not possibly be consuming all that seed and that their population had not increased, while the squirrel population had. The next morning confirmed her observation as I watched a squirrel shinny down the wire to help itself to the bird feeder while two of its companions perched on the limb above, awaiting their turn.

Naturally I assumed that I could quickly outwit these furry little thieves. I nailed the bird feeder to the top of a tall pole far from the nearest tree. The squirrels promptly scampered up the pole. I coated it with grease, in the process ruining a shirt and a pair of pants. The squirrels still climbed the pole and now found that they could slide down more easily after consuming all the seed. Meanwhile, flocks of birds sat on the empty feeder, regarding our back door with reproach. But the birds were already forgotten; I was concentrating on my contest with the squirrels.

A neighbor recommended a metal dome suspended halfway down the wire of a hanging bird feeder. I tried it and was gratified to see a couple of squirrels baffled by the obstruction. But not for long. A few days later I watched as a squirrel paced back and forth on the limb above the protected feeder, twitching its tail as it studied the obstruction and considered how to overcome it. The solution apparently came in a flash, because the squirrel suddenly grasped the wire and swung the feeder back and forth until most of its seeds were dumped on the ground, where three more squirrels joined the feast.

Collecting what wits I had left, I considered the fact that I knew the least about the animal I was seeing the most, and retreated to the local library. It took only a little research to confirm that the squirrel, a member of the rodent family (ranging from mice to beavers), is indeed the most numerous of all mammals. It inhabits every landmass except Australia, Madagascar, and the polar regions. It comes in a vast variety of species, including some that are large, fat, and lazy and others that glide from tree to tree; gray squirrels that build separate winter and summer homes; and ferocious little red squirrels that often drive away gray squirrels twice their size. (Not so, apparently, in England, where the Forestry Authority has asked for governmental approval to trap and even poison "foreign" gray squirrels that the authority claims are harassing the native red squirrels to extinction.)

The suburban squirrel I was dealing with is the Eastern gray *(Sciurus carolinensis)*, which is the species best known to most Americans from northeastern Canada to the southeastern United States and as far west as the Great Plains; a couple of close cousins, the Western and California grays, inhabit most of the western states.

Taxonomists divide the North American tree squirrels

by their physical characteristics into more than fifty species and hundreds of subspecies. But I found that a more logical, if less scientific, division can be made by behavior: country squirrels, city squirrels, and suburban squirrels. Country squirrels are wild and wary; city squirrels are unabashedly tame; suburban squirrels are in between and seem to have the best of both worlds. They have fewer wild predators than do their country cousins and face fewer man-made dangers (such as traffic, pollution, and too many humans) than do the city squirrels.

All of them, as I had already begun to realize, are highly intelligent little animals. The gray squirrel, I read, has an abnormally large brain case. (I could have guessed that.) Country squirrels can sidle around a tree so cleverly that a predator doesn't even know they are there. City squirrels rob vending machines (by reaching in the back); they have also been seen waiting for a red light before crossing the street. Not only are suburban squirrels masters at robbing bird feeders, but they also watch television and enjoy music; one ingenious panhandler even faked a limp to elicit more handouts.

A thirsty squirrel, finding a bowl of ice, sat on it until it melted, then drank its fill. A neighbor of mine trapped two squirrels in a box, took them to the nearest park, and released them; he swears that they were back the same day. Indeed, the pioneering naturalist John C. Muir agreed that squirrels had an uncanny homing instinct. "It is not well understood by science," he wrote, "but they will often return several miles." One squirrel lover submitted as evidence of the animal's intelligence that there were an inordinate number of squirrels in Harvard Yard; on the other hand, there is a particularly large squirrel population around the White House. (One naturalist claims that in Lafayette Park, across Pennsylvania Avenue from the

White House, "the density of squirrels . . . is the highest ever recorded in the scientific literature.")

Nonetheless, evidence of their intelligence is found nearly everywhere squirrels live. City squirrels quickly discover that apartment flowerpots are handy for burying their nuts, causing consternation when some of them sprout into small trees. A New York City couple who invited a squirrel into their apartment were soon hosts to a dozen of its companions. The squirrels called every day and quickly adjusted to apartment life. A ringing telephone startled them once but not thereafter—though they never got over being fascinated by their host's back exercises. They peremptorily tapped their host or hostess on the leg or shoulder when the nut feeder needed replenishing. Every morning they announced their arrival by banging on the window—but only after courteously waiting for signs of life in the apartment.

Their hostess, a physicist, discovered that these squirrels had mastered a basic law of physics: they would jump *up* to a precarious perch (in this case her fire-escape railing) but never *down* to it, somehow knowing that a projectile moves at its slowest rate of speed at the top of its parabolic course and at its fastest on the way down.

Other city dwellers have found that squirrels have adapted readily to the human habitat of roofs, power lines, and fire escapes. One urbanite watched in fascination as a squirrel descended to the ground from his fifteenth-floor window by leaping from one air conditioner to another, some of them four floors apart.

Though the squirrel's preferred food is nuts, its stomach has adjusted to bagels as well as birdseed, Cracker Jack and cough drops, lettuce and larvae, tea and tubers, pizza, pancakes, and peanut butter. One donor watched a squirrel gulp down a large gob of peanut butter that stuck in its throat. For almost a full minute the squirrel stood nearly comatose, its eyes half closed, until the peanut butter dissolved, whereupon it calmly gobbled up another helping.

Evidently a favorite nut is the macadamia, as attested to by a neighbor of mine. When a squirrel joined a cocktail party on his patio, a guest tossed it a macadamia nut. The squirrel nibbled on it tentatively, blinked its eyes, swallowed it with obvious satisfaction, then ran over and put its paw on its benefactor's leg, apparently as if to say, "Now *that's* what I call a *nut!*"

The squirrel's teeth are perfectly formed for cracking the shells of its favorite food with great efficiency. One evening our neighbors left a large bag of nuts at our door. By early morning there was nothing but a pile of shells. The gray squirrel has no canines, but possesses strong grinding molars that can move forward, backward, and from side to side. In fact, the molars must be kept at work grinding against one another or they will grow too long. The rare unfortunate squirrel with malocclusion may kill itself as its molars inexorably grow inward and pierce its brain.

A lesser menace to the squirrel is what most well-wishers feed it. Peanuts might seem to be the ideal squirrel food, but peanuts alone do not provide the proper nourishment. As long ago as 1908, a *Forest and Stream* magazine article described the plight of park squirrels in Harrisburg, Pennsylvania, that were being fed peanuts by well-meaning strollers. The magazine reported that "it was not long until their fur got thin and ragged, and they became mangy and sickly." Park personnel urged the substitution of pecans and walnuts, and shortly the squirrels' fur became "thick and glossy, and their tails bushy and luxuriant."

Despite its name, the gray squirrel's fur is tan with shades of black; its underparts are white and its tail is tipped with black. (Some genetic variations, especially in the north, are pure black. There are also rare albino grays.) The gray squirrel's fur changes with the seasons, molting from front to back in the spring and from back to front in the fall, when it is replaced by denser fur for the winter. Russian squirrel fur is particularly dense, and the best squirrel coats are made from Russian pelts. The squirrel does not hibernate but does lie up in its den, protected by its thick fur, during snowstorms.

About twenty inches long and weighing a little less than a pound, the gray squirrel has bulging eyes set in the side of its head, providing wide peripheral vision. Its eyesight is so keen that it can spot a nut on the ground from high in a tree; but it cannot see dead ahead at close range. So, when it approaches the nut, it has to rely on its highly developed sense of smell. For this reason squirrels frequently, though innocently, bite the hands that feed them.

The squirrel's tiny triangular ears are also acute; some northern species grow little tufts on their ears in winter to protect them from the cold. Between its toes are its only sweat glands. Like a cat, the squirrel has sensitive nose whiskers to tell it when an opening is too small for its body. Its prehensile paws can cling to almost any surface; but, unlike a cat's, the claws do not retract, so the squirrel has to run on sidewalks, driveways, and other hard surfaces on its heels.

The marvel of squirrel evolution is its magnificent tail, which in most species is about half the length of the animal's body. Its uses are almost infinite. It serves as a rudder when the squirrel is darting along the ground, twisting and turning with lightning speed. The squirrel's tail also guides it as it jumps from one tree to another. It acts as a sort of parachute on the rare occasion when the squirrel tumbles, twitching back and forth to lessen the speed of its fall. A pet squirrel visiting a New York hotel with its owners fell sixteen floors down an air shaft and suffered only a nosebleed.

Some early naturalists credited the squirrel's tail with being the first sail, claiming occasionally to have seen a squirrel, confronted with a body of water, launch a piece of wood, climb on, spread its tail to the breeze, and sail across.

In winter, when the squirrel curls up in its den, it uses its tail as a blanket; in summer its tail is a parasol. (*Sciurus* means "shade of tail.") Rain does not drive a squirrel to cover; it simply holds its tail over its body, flicking away the raindrops as they fall. One woman claims to have seen a dainty squirrel finish eating, grasp its tail with its forepaws, and use it to whisk the crumbs from its mouth.

For its home, the squirrel prefers a hole in a tree. Some gray squirrels also build a summer home, usually a nest in a high tree crotch. It is an elaborate globular construction on a platform of twigs. Unlike a bird's nest, it has a roof. Woven like a basket, the nest weighs about six pounds, is waterproof, and has an inner room lined with shredded bark, leaves, grass, moss, and salvaged paper and cloth; one squirrel used pieces of the miniature flags in a nearby cemetery. The nest door usually faces inward, next to the tree trunk or a limb. Since squirrels are hosts to innumerable vermin, including lice, fleas, and mites, they simply move out when the nest becomes infested.

I had noticed that there seemed to be more squirrels about in the morning and late afternoon. This, I found, was because the suburban gray squirrel likes its siesta. It is up before dawn and retires to its nest at about noon. My parents inadvertently persuaded one squirrel to put off its siesta by feeding it at noon each day. When they forgot, the squirrel politely tapped on their patio door to remind them that it was lunchtime. Usually a squirrel comes out again for supper near dusk; on clear, moonlit nights it may continue foraging into the late hours, whether it is hungry or not. And therein lies a famous squirrel legend.

It is a common belief that squirrels spend the autumn months industriously burying food for the winter, and that when the squirrels are particularly busy through the fall, it will be a bitter winter. Squirrels do tend to eat more at this time of year to store up fat for the winter. But busy autumn squirrels do not necessarily predict an especially cold winter. Smart as they are, they are not weather forecasters; they are just as ravenous preceding a mild winter. Moreover, squirrels spend the entire year burying food—after they have eaten enough to keep them fat and happy. A healthy squirrel can consume an amount that in a human would be fifteen thousand calories a day. (Normal daily human intake is about two thousand calories.) What the squirrel can't eat, it buries, in an elaborate process.

First it shakes the nutshell and listens to make sure there is a nut inside. Then it usually checks to see if the shell is broken; a buried nut with a cracked shell will spoil or start growing into a tree. Satisfied that it is worth preserving, the squirrel takes the nut in its mouth, selects a burial site, and digs a shallow hole with its forepaws. It drops the nut into the hole, scrapes dirt over it, tamps it down, and goes back for more. Occasionally a lazy squirrel may not dig a hole but simply cover the nut with a few leaves. The squirrels in our yard also sometimes stash a partly eaten apple or ear of corn in the crotch of a tree, returning when they are hungry again to finish it.

So strong is the squirrel's burying instinct that the New York woman mentioned previously who invited squirrels into her home found them burying nuts in all the flower pots in her apartment. When she retrieved what she could find, one smart squirrel took to faking two or three burials to confuse her search.

For centuries, amateur naturalists pondered the question: How does the squirrel remember where it has planted its food? We now know the answer. It does not. In the course of a year a squirrel buries thousands of nuts, so its habitat is larded with buried food. And with its superb sense of smell, the squirrel simply noses about until it detects a nut and digs it up. One naturalist saw a squirrel sniff a nut through a foot of snow and dig straight down to retrieve it. Since most squirrels are nonterritorial, the nut may well have been planted by another neighborhood squirrel.

So a lot of nuts get buried never to be dug up again. Thus, in nature's way, many of these nuts eventually become trees, and the squirrel thereby inadvertently helps reforest its environment with the very trees it prefers.

Not only that. The famous naturalist Ernest Thompson Seton pointed out that the nuts the gray squirrel most often buries are hickory, butternut, and walnut. The acorn, Seton observed, falls to the ground and, if not eaten, seeds itself to become an oak tree. But the hickory, butternut, and walnut must first be buried. So, Seton argued, most of the forests in North America owe their existence to the gray squirrel.

Meanwhile, the squirrels are busy propagating their own species. The ones I have seen romping about in early spring are males on the make; and what I thought to be games of tag are frequently contests for the favors of a female. Although I've never noticed it (perhaps because suburban squirrels are more polite), males battling for supremacy can fill the air with their screams and cut each other up savagely. To the winner goes the female, thus ensuring that the strongest of the species propagate. The

naturalist Vernon Bailey delicately describes the procedure: "Wild, free gray squirrels do not pair except for a day and a night, or at most two days and two nights, until the female is satisfied and the male exhausted and glad to go away and rest up."

One reason is that the male may shortly be called on for a second or third mating if there is plenty of food available. But in a marvel of nature, squirrels may pass up the breeding season entirely if food is scarce. Another marvel is the way the pregnant female squirrel is prevented from later mating with an inferior male. After copulation, the dominant male excretes a waxy substance that forms a plug to block the female's vagina, like a chastity belt, until she produces her young.

While the male retires to bachelor quarters, the female gestates for a little over forty days. Her litter ranges from three to five pups—naked, blind, weighing about an ounce, with unformed ears and stumps for feet. Not for a month will their eyes open and their fur begin to sprout. But then they grow fast; within a couple of weeks they are venturing out on a limb under their mother's supervision. By now their tails have grown bushy to help them parachute if they blunder off the limb. They remain with their mother until summer, when she may mate again. If, in the meantime, she needs to move them, she grasps them one at a time and, while the baby squirrel hangs on with its legs around her neck, carries it to her new home. When her second birth approaches, she leaves the winter home to her first litter and moves to her summer nest for a second brood in September. By now her firstborn are quite able to function on their own.

Young and old communicate with a wide repertoire of sounds: the familiar chirp, the *qua, qua, qua* that resembles a duck's quack, a clucking sound as the squirrel goes its rounds, the angry chatter of gnashing teeth (accompanied by twitching tail language), the purr of satisfaction, the crooning of a courting male. One human suburbanite listened in admiration as a couple of crooning squirrels attracted a flock of sparrows that occasionally joined the chorus.

The squirrel's chirp caused a small problem a few years ago in Davis, California, where traffic engineers made the mistake of installing a traffic light with a chirping beeper. A local squirrel, chirping in response, caused utter confusion among the blind pedestrians for whom the beeper was intended.

Young squirrels are taught how to evade their many predators—hawks, owls, snakes, weasels, foxes, raccoons, dogs, cats, and man. The squirrel's most effective defense is flight. A nimble squirrel sidling around a tree trunk can drive a circling hawk to exasperation. With its powerful hind legs, a squirrel can jump six feet into the air and as much as eight feet between tree branches. The fastest squirrel was clocked at almost twenty miles an hour. At that speed it cannot outrun a long-legged dog on the straightaway, but it easily eludes pursuers with bewildering evasive action. One naturalist claimed that the only time he ever saw a squirrel caught by dogs was when one tumbled from a tree between two of them. This could have been after an ice storm, which makes tree limbs too slick even for a squirrel. The other great danger to the squirrel is the automobile, which, as every driver knows, seems to drive the animal berserk.

The squirrel was here long before the automobile; one fossil has been dated at more than 30 million years old. American squirrels happily subsisted on the unlimited supply of nuts provided by the vast forests of early America; in those days it was said that a squirrel could travel from the East Coast to the Mississippi River without touching the ground.

When the first settlers arrived and planted corn, the squirrels promptly devoured it. There were a lot of squirrels in North America in those days, and their numbers continued to increase. Ernest Thompson Seton estimated that by 1800 the North American squirrel population approached one billion, a number that threatened overpopulation and led to a series of squirrel migrations from overcrowded regions during the nineteenth century.

In 1849 the naturalist John Bachman described one lemminglike mass movement in the Northwest: "Onward they come, devouring on the way everything that is suited to their taste, laying waste the corn and wheat fields of the farmer." Another naturalist estimated that some fifty thousand squirrels crossed the Allegheny Mountains in one day. And another reported seeing such a packed mass of the migrating animals that some were forced to leapfrog over others. One swarm, fleeing a shortage of nut trees in southern Wisconsin, even swam across the Mississippi to the Iowa side. Fishermen claimed to have watched hordes of them gathering on the east bank to wait for calm weather before striking out across the river. The swimming squirrel usually employs a modified dog paddle, with its head and tail out of the water.

American hunters were meanwhile doing their part to reduce the squirrel population. In one 1804 squirrel hunt, two thousand were killed in a single day. The Columbus, Ohio, *Gazette* reported in August of 1822 a slaughter to protect nearby grainfields, in which some twenty thousand squirrels were shot in three days.

Squirrel hunters also progagated what became a popular myth. Noticing that many of their male victims seemed to have no testes, they concluded that in mating battles the victor castrated the loser. Zoologists have since discovered, however, that between mating periods the male squirrel's testes are hidden in his abdomen, descending to his scrotum only when his hormones signal that it is breeding time again.

By the end of the nineteenth century, with squirrel hunting still popular and squirrel habitat diminished by logging, environmentalists were predicting the extinction of the species. (A two-day West Virginia hunt in 1909 bagged only three victims.) Squirrel pie and baked squirrel were regarded as delicacies. But the squirrel survived man's guns—with some help from belated state hunting restrictions—and learned to adapt to the rapidly changing environment. By the 1920s, Seton calculated that there were still 15 million of them in North America; today the number is in the high millions.

Because the suburbs have few of its former predators, a healthy squirrel has about a fifteen-year life span. As it ages, it grows some gray hairs and may develop cataracts; but it remains nearly as frisky as ever. Under coddled conditions, one pet squirrel lived to the venerable age of twenty.

The squirrel does not live by nuts alone. It obviously enjoys life, and even has an antic sense of humor. The squirrels in our neighborhood take perverse pleasure in teasing the local dogs and cats, streaking just ahead of them to the nearest tree, where, from a safe distance, they deliver a taunting chatter. Our son-in-law reports that on a fishing trip he was awakened every morning by squirrels happily sliding down his tent. A New York game warden who tamed a squirrel found that it enjoyed sitting on his shoulder watching television; it particularly liked professional wrestling.

But evidently one of the animal's most intriguing adaptations to humans is its love of music. The naturalist C. Merriam Hart reported that a squirrel hearing a musical instrument or recording often drops whatever it is eating, stands upright, and leans forward, moving its head from side to side in rapt absorption as it listens to the melody. Merriam had one squirrel whose favorite tune was "Just Before the Battle, Mother"; whenever Merriam whistled this tune, "in as pathetic a tone as I could muster," the squirrel let him approach and pet it, responding with "a low purring sound" of pure contentment. Yet another squirrel watcher discovered that they may have selective musical taste; he drove an invading colony out of his attic by playing loud rock music. But evidently not all squirrels are so discerning. One squirrel owner claims that hers "is not even moved by Mozart."

There are those who regard the squirrel as a mixed blessing. Utility company managers get upset when a squirrel shorts out an electric line (though not as upset as the squirrel, which is instantly electrocuted). The squirrel finds the metal in the cables useful for grinding down its molars. In Clifton, New Jersey, some years ago, one squirrel cut off power to 35,000 homes and factories. The Washington, D.C., area once had seven blackouts in one day caused by squirrels.

Squirrels often carry rabies and can infect humans by blindly biting their hands. Squirrels can also be petty thieves: a tourist in the Brooklyn Botanic Gardens who had photographed a squirrel made the mistake of putting down his camera for a moment; his subject nipped down from the tree and ran off with the camera. Those who are old enough to remember the famous Buick models with small portholes in the hood can sympathize with the Buick owner who was baffled by an unholy noise in his engine until he found that squirrels had been hiding nuts in the holes.

Squirrels gnawing their way into houses cause untold damage. A New Jersey suburbanite returned home one evening to find that a squirrel had broken in, opened a bottle of Scotch, and was still drunkenly lapping it up. A frequent homeowner's problem is a squirrel invasion of the attic, where they are extremely difficult to dislodge. One Ohio woman attempting to drive a squirrel from her attic retreated under a barrage of Christmas-tree ornaments.

But it is the great American army of some 80 million bird lovers who are most frustrated, challenged, and outwitted by the suburban gray squirrel. They spend some $500 million a year on birdseed, much of which is eaten by squirrels. Birders' magazines are full of ingenious and intricate "squirrel-proof" feeders; more than a dozen patents have been taken out for such devices. One victim of squirrel raids was moved to write a book titled *Outwitting Squirrels*, in which he listed more than a hundred strategies. Most of the defenses are only temporarily successful. Squirrels slither over feeder covers, tightrope-walk across wires, and leap seemingly impossible distances. A friend reported the incredible agility of a local squirrel so successful and well fed that he called it "Fat Charley." Charley, confronted with my friend's hooded bird feeder, simply flew from the nearest tree trunk to land under the hood. Another bird lover attempted to counter the feeder robbers by bombing them with water bags.

Nonetheless, the squirrel has many defenders, if only because of its frolicking activity and death-defying leaps from tree to tree. It was a historian, however, who claimed what must have been the squirrel's greatest contribution to its fellow Americans. The squirrel was one of the most difficult targets for early marksmen, not only because of its evasive action but because it could flatten itself against a tree to become nearly invisible. As a result, early American squirrel hunters became the best sharpshooters in the world. And during the American Revolution it was the Minuteman with his squirrel rifle who picked off, one by one, the British soldiers trained to advance in ranks.

Not long after my unequal contest with the robbers of my bird feeder, I happened to visit a friend with an aptitude for engineering who had finally defeated the squirrels in his Pennsylvania yard. He had fashioned an elaborate bird feeder with a metal grid and a wire carrying an electric charge. The grid was balanced by a spring mechanism that accepted the weight of a few birds but sagged under the weight of a squirrel to make contact with the electric wire; the charge sent the squirrel flying every time.

That was just what I needed. I returned home determined to copy it. But the more I thought about those
intelligent little critters that tease dogs, save food for days
of need, have reforested America—and even helped win
our independence—the more I realized that they deserve
all the bird seed they can get. Besides, as my wife politely
reminded me, I never would have mastered that intricate
squirrel-shocker anyway.

So now I feed the squirrels. In fact, I found in a catalog
an ingenious squirrel feeder consisting of a wooden seat
alongside a spike that holds an ear of corn. The squirrel
contentedly sits on the seat and stuffs itself to near stupefac-
tion with corn. Indeed, the manufacturer of this device
claims that with a squirrel feeder in one corner of a surbur-
ban lot, the squirrels will leave the bird feeders alone.

Another catalog offers another squirrel feeder, this
one designed to challenge the critter's acrobatic ability. It
consists of a long chain with a spike at the end. You stick
an ear of corn on the spike, hook the chain over a tree limb,
and watch the fun. It proved to be no challenge to our
squirrels, who studied it only for a day. By the next day,
when I looked out the window, it was gone. The squirrels
had unhooked the chain and let it drop to the ground,
where they had finished off the corn; then they had left the
chain at my door for a refill.

Meanwhile, they enjoy their feeder and the bird feeders alike. But the birds seem to survive on the seeds the
squirrels scatter. The small birds, that is—because I apparently have a new problem. For all its high IQ and agility,
the gray squirrel tends to be a coward. We have a feisty
mockingbird, a couple of ferocious blue jays, and some
crows that regularly drive the squirrels away from their
feeder. I've got to do something about those birds.

FOUR

Canada Geese on the Lawn

ONE of my favorite nature writers is Henry Hill Collins, Jr., if only because of his rich, rolling prose. Here, Collins is moved to poetic rapture by migrating Canada geese:

> As the clarion notes float downward on the still night air, who can resist the temptation to rush out of doors and peer into the darkness for a possible glimpse at the passing flock, as the shadowy forms glide over our roofs on the long journey? Or, even in daylight, what man so busy that he will not pause and look upward at the serried ranks of our grandest wild fowl, as their well-known honking notes announce their coming and their going, he knows not whence or whither? . . . Certainly the Canada goose commands respect.

That was thirty years ago. It is no longer the case, at least not in our neighborhood. We have no need of looking to the sky to see the local Canada geese; they are all over the place. Most of my neighbors may regard them with respect, but only because of the Canada's shrewd decision to quit all that flying way up north and way down south—

a decision that has made the Canada goose a lot less popular in Greenwich, Connecticut, than it was to Mr. Collins a generation ago.

Migration, ornithologists say, is essential to the life of many birds. Moving north and south with the seasons, genetically programmed to follow the sun and fly by the stars, ducks, egrets, and even sandpipers travel thousands of miles a year. I remember marveling to a scientist friend at the phenomenon of the tiny sandpiper flying all the way to South America and returning to our cove every year. His answer was pragmatic. "What else have they got to do? They have plenty of time," he said. "Do you expect them to spend it lounging at the beach?"

But that, in effect, is what the Canada geese have learned to do. Instead of migrating, they have settled in on our coves, ponds, beaches, parks, and golf courses for the rest of their lives. When the ducks wing by in autumn and spring, our Canada geese don't bother to look up at them. Migration is the farthest thing from their sharp little minds. They have no idea where Canada is, or that it even exists, and they couldn't care less. They are perfectly content to lounge on the beach or float about the cove. In winter or summer they parade contentedly about their suburban domain, cropping the grass, honking at cars, cadging treats from toddlers, and fouling the ground with their cigarette-sized droppings.

Most of our Canada geese are fifth- and sixth-generation immigrants. Instead of the corn and wheat their ancestors foraged for, these geese prefer sandwiches, doughnuts, and Dove Bars. Instead of struggling for existence on the lonely tundras of the north in summer or the marshes of the Carolinas in winter, they prefer picnics. And when they fly at all, they bear little resemblance to the high-soaring V formation so admired by naturalist Collins; instead they barely clear our housetops in a ragged flight pattern, their feet dangling as they honk their way from cove to pond.

Ornithologists seem to agree that the Canada goose is one of the more intelligent species of birds. Certainly ours are, having recognized before we did that our neighborhood provides the perfect goose habitat. Our parks and golf courses (Greenwich has eight golf courses) offer the combination of close-mown grass, with its nutritious green shoots, and plenty of bushes for their nests, all of it near a pond, a lake, or Long Island Sound. And to make it even easier, there are plenty of suburbanites ever ready to supplement the goose's natural diet with handouts.

Evidently not as bright as the geese, some of my neighbors, captivated by the sight of a couple of these handsome, white-cheeked birds, welcomed them with bread crumbs— and complained a few weeks later when their lawn swarmed with the critters. An occasional sight at one of Greenwich's parks is a limousine that stops for the chauffeur to toss grain to the geese while the lady of the manor watches approvingly from the car.

In fact, some of my friends contend that our geese have adapted so well that during election years more of them attend Republican than Democratic picnics, knowing well which party dominates local politics and thus the regulations for the town's beaches and parks. (I'm inclined to doubt this; a more likely explanation is that the food is better at the Republican picnics.)

Provided with the perfect habitat, coddled by the human residents, protected from most predators, our geese, not surprisingly, have multiplied prodigiously. An official estimate of their population in the state was five thousand— until it was drastically altered when an Audubon Christmas bird count recorded 32,594 Canada geese. And while some of my neighbors are convinced that all 32,594 of them reside in Greenwich, the best estimate for our town is about 1,500, which expands to five thousand when seasonal visitors drop in from the north. Among those Canadas that still migrate, many "short-stop," as the ornithologists describe it, instead of proceeding farther south as they are supposed to—especially in Greenwich when (like the rest of us) they find the town to their liking.

Even five thousand, in a town with sixty thousand people, is a lot of geese. And since it takes only six geese to defecate roughly the same amount as one human, it's also a lot of goose-doo. One of my friends, in what might be called tragic pentameter, complained:

> Canada goose, with bowels so loose,
> Forgo my pondside lawn, oh please!

Sunbathers complain that there are few clean places to lay a beach towel. Golfers skid on the greens, and course attendants complain that their lawnmowers get gummed up with goose droppings and their drains clogged with feathers. Water hazards are turning green with goose excrement. Toddlers in the parks are befouled; although local hygienists claim that no one has been made ill by them, goose droppings can contain salmonella. When improvements were made to the local sewage system, town officials announced that our long-closed clamming beds would be reopened, only to have to reverse the order because rainstorms washed goose droppings into the cove and repolluted it.

Once wary in the wild, Canada geese have adapted quickly to our nonthreatening neighborhood. They are tame—some say arrogant—enough to harass sunbathers for sandwiches and snatch cookies out of children's hands. They take dips in the local swimming pools. They eat golf fairways down to stubble. During the breeding season they attack hikers and bike riders who happen near their nests. Traffic is occasionally tied up by geese crossing the road. So perhaps it is not surprising that our parks and recreation director, Frank Keegan, angrily refers to them as "thirty-five-pound pigeons" and "flying rats."

Greenwich is not alone. Canada geese have taken up year-round residence in suburbs all across the temperate climate zone of the United States. Farther south, in the Carolinas, the southern destination of Canada geese in earlier times, environmentalists (and especially hunters) bemoan the fact that the 200,000 Canadas that wintered there in the 1950s have dwindled to fifty thousand. Meanwhile, in New Jersey and New York, wildlife experts calculate that the Canada goose population has risen in one decade from only a few to some ninety thousand. The manager of a golf course in a Buffalo suburb complained that he couldn't find a spot free of goose droppings to put down his golf bag. The mayor of Long Island's Glen Cove, who had authorized a short, supervised hunt to lower the goose population, complained, "I am up to my neck in geese, and some people are mad at me because I allowed a few of them to be shot. The golfers are mad at me because I won't shoot any more. The only ones who aren't mad at anybody are the geese. They're still here."

In a New Jersey suburb a mother complained, "My children have to shoo them away when they go outside," and she has had to make the kids leave their shoes at the door when they come in. A nearby housewife claimed, "It got so bad, if you drove up the driveway, you'd discolor your tires. The slime was awful."

Apparently a few smart geese decided to short-stop some time ago. In the mid-nineteenth century, John James Audubon wrote, "Although the Canada goose is considered a northern species, the number of individuals that remain at all seasons in the milder latitudes, and in different portions of the United States, fully entitles this bird to be looked upon as a permanent resident there." Audubon and some other ornithologists prompted me to do my own amateur study of Canada geese.

They are also called, in various parts of the United States, honkers, yelpers, bay geese, black-necked geese, northern geese, reef geese, wild geese, ringnecks, and white-cheeked geese. My birdwatcher friends tell me never to call them Canadian geese, but they can't tell me why. The scientific name is *Branta canadensis*. *Branta* comes from a Greek word for "bird," and *canadensis* is Latin for "Canadian." Taxonomists class our bird in the order of the Anseriformes (Latin for "goose") and the family of web-footed swimming Anatidae. *Branta* is its genus and *canadensis* its species. There is a lot of argument about the number of subspecies, but the best estimate is eleven, ranging from the giant Canada to the duck-sized cackling Canada.

Ours is called *Branta canadensis canadensis* to distinguish it as the subspecies preferring the Atlantic flyway (as opposed to the other three major flyways, Mississippi, Central, and Pacific). Those that have settled in Greenwich should weigh about fifteen to twenty pounds, but most of them are bigger than that. Some ornithologists claim that these nonmigrating birds are in fact a new subspecies of the rare giant Canada *(Branta canadensis maxima)*, the largest of them all, with a six-foot wingspread. Indeed, some of our local Canadas are so fat that they can scarcely stagger into the water. They may be a giant subspecies or simply overfed to the point of obesity. No doubt a good thousand-mile migration would slim them down.

Their ancestors seem to have first appeared some 500

million years ago. The American Indians, in their tepees where our houses now stand, presumably saw Canada geese only in the fall and spring, during their migrations along the Atlantic flyway. But even with bow and arrow they made good use of them as they came through. Roast goose is as nutritious as it is delicious. Goose feathers warmed many an Indian's bed. And goose grease, because of its quick penetration, was an early panacea for everything from rheumatism to the common cold. White settlers liked the taste of Canada goose so much that they trapped them (sometimes with whiskey-soaked corn) and fattened them for holiday dinners.

So maybe it's time to pay the geese back with the loan of our parks and beaches. Walking among them as they strut along our beach, I get the sense that they think so too. The Canada goose, I read, is more ambulatory than most birds; its legs are set closer to the center of the body than those of the waddling duck or the hopping robin. And with its long, regal neck, the critter strikes a lordly, not to say arrogant, pose.

I'm struck by their similarities to swans. Like swans, Canada geese are monogamous; and as with swans, there is occasional adultery or polygamy. Unlike mallards, for example, the gander and his mate look alike; but the gander knows the difference. Audubon gives a colorful description of the mating of the Canada goose, the gander advancing on his intended mate, "his head scarcely raised an inch from the ground, his bill open to its full stretch, his fleshy tongue elevated, his eyes darting fiery glances." Hissing with passion, his feathers and quills rustling, he prances around her, gently touching her. As she "acknowledges his affection, they move their necks in a hundred curious ways."

But frequently the idyll is interrupted by a contending

gander. I have seen one or two of these confrontations, but never one like the scene witnessed by Audubon. The attacking gander advances on the lovers, Audubon writes, "his eye glowing with the fire of rage. . . . The whole flock seems to stand amazed, and opening up a space, the birds gather round to view the combat." The battle comes to a quick conclusion: "now the mated gander has caught hold of his antagonist's head with his bill; no bull-dog could cling faster to his victim; he squeezes him with all the energy of rage, lashes him with his powerful wings, and at length drives him away, spreads out his pinions, runs with joy to his mate and fills the air with cries of exultation."

If the victor's mate-to-be, suitably impressed by his prowess, is ready to accept him, she fluffs her feathers and may mince away for a few steps and wait for him to catch up. He approaches her again with neck outstretched, head swaying back and forth and feathers ruffled. And then he starts to snore.

That, the ornithologists say, is what really attracts her; snoring is the ultimate sign of his intention. Shortly they are entwining necks. The gander turns and prances toward the nearest water. She follows him. Here the foreplay picks up its pace, with much head-dipping, both tossing water over their backs and each other. After a couple minutes of splashing, she stretches her long neck out as the signal.

I remember the alarm with which I first watched the culmination of this courtship, convinced that one goose was drowning the other. Almost entirely submerged by his weight for about half a minute, she quickly surfaced when he moved away, both splashing again as they raised their necks triumphantly, flapped their wings, and circled each other, the gander snoring even more loudly. Within minutes they returned to land and stood together preening themselves.

The gander and his mate are usually three years old or older, though a few can breed at two. Most will remain mates for life, breeding every spring and raising each family through the summer.

The female of the species decides where the nest will be. During their western explorations in 1805, Lewis and Clark reported finding a Canada goose nest high atop a cottonwood tree. A few others have been known to select lofty sites, sometimes appropriating nests of other large birds; one Canada goose was found in a blue heron's nest, incubating her own eggs and those of the heron. But usually the Canada mother-to-be chooses something on firm ground, preferably obscured by high grass and near the water. One practical goose built her nest in an abandoned tire; another used a discarded laundry tub.

With little help from her gander, she collects bits of grass, straw, twigs, pine needles, and anything else she can carry in her beak. Squatting in a depression in the ground, she assembles the nest around her until the sides are a few inches high. The nests I've seen were about four inches deep and thirty inches in diameter. A fussy housewife, she continues to tidy up the nest throughout her incubation period. Unlike many other birds, which foul their nests, the Canada goose keeps hers clean; many a golfer or beachgoer wishes she were as neat elsewhere.

The eggs—an average of five, off-white and about three inches by two inches—take just under a month to incubate. During that time the mother goose cushions them with down plucked from her breast; by the time they are ready to hatch, she has bared a part of her chest (called the "incubation patch"), and her bare skin helps keep the eggs at her body temperature, about one hundred degrees. She also uses the down to cover them when she has to leave the nest. Periodically she uses her bill to turn the eggs, both to

provide uniform temperature and to prevent the mem-
branes of the embryos from adhering to the shell.

Unlike the swan, the Canada gander does not cover
the eggs during his mate's brief absences, which rarely last
more than an hour, especially as hatching time approaches.
The gander is meanwhile on twenty-four-hour guard duty,
hissing and honking at any intruder. Canada goose eggs
attract skunks, raccoons, gulls, crows, and dogs, but few
are a match for a Canada gander stubbornly defending his
incubating brood. When I once happened upon a nest, I
was warned off by the earsplitting din of the honking gander and his yelping mate. They were not bluffing. The
Canada goose's wings are strong and tipped with knobby
bones that can beat a small trespasser to death. Audubon
reported that when he came too close to a nest, the gander
nearly broke his arm; he was unable to use it for a week.
Another gander fought to the death defending his nest, in
the process knocking a two-hundred-pound intruder off
his horse.

Usually near the end of April, our goslings are ready
to hatch. They announce their imminent arrival a couple of
days early by chirping inside the shells. Shortly each one,
its beak temporarily armed with what is called an "egg
tooth," is poking its way out. Within twenty-four hours
all of the goslings are staggering about the nest, sodden but
already open-eyed and covered with down. The sex ratio,
unlike that of mammals, is usually fifty-fifty. While their
mother carefully disposes of the shells, the goslings scurry
about until their downy coats are dry.

This is the point at which they are "imprinted," or
psychologically attached to their parents. As Konrad Lorenz proved in his famous experiments, geese, ducks, and
similar birds attach themselves to the first thing they see,
in his case Lorenz himself, following him around convinced

that he was their parent. I use the word "thing" advisedly; in Greenwich Cove a Canada gosling, straying from its nest in the first few hours, attached itself to a sailboat and swam about in the boat's wake, evidently believing itself to be a dinghy. Normally, however, the goslings immediately attach themselves to their proper parents, who promptly lead them to the nearest water, never to return to their nest again.

Canada goslings are nudifugous, i.e., ready to walk, swim, and eat as soon as they are born. In a straight line, with the gander in the lead and the mother bringing up the rear, the family moves out onto the pond or cove, away from the dangers on land. And in case the downy goslings might present too much of a temptation to a gull or hawk, their parents teach them how to dive for cover. Even a gosling can swim as far as forty feet under water, and a Canada can remain submerged for an hour or more with only the tip of its beak out of the water to breathe. The parents also show their newborn how to tip up like ducks, reaching under the water to nibble the bottom grasses with their sharp bills. Only when the goslings are acclimated does the family go ashore to forage among the reeds for most of its food.

Canada geese in rural areas tend to maintain their nuclear families, keeping apart from the others. But in our suburban neighborhood the families intermingle. On my walks along the shore I usually encounter such a gathering, two or three sets of goslings cropping the beach grass alongside their parents, accompanied by their uncles, aunts, cousins, and grandparents. In each group a couple of geese stand watch, heads up, on the lookout for any danger. If I approach them, one of the sentinels may hiss at me; just as frequently one will advance to check me out for food. If I have nothing to offer, it struts away, shaking its head, and the rest follow. If another beach-walker is accompanied by his dog, the geese go snorting into the water. And if the dog follows, they take wing, honking in annoyance. Wheeling over our heads, they fly farther down the beach to a safer spot. Everyone has marveled at the spectacle of migrating Canada geese flying in precise V formation. Not our geese. Since they are simply hopping from one local area to another, they have no need to assemble in formation as they do in higher-altitude flying. Our geese may even have forgotten how.

Canada goslings are voracious feeders. Within a month of birth, each weighs about three pounds; by a month later it is twenty-four times birth size. A human baby growing at this rate would weigh more than 150 pounds at eight weeks. The goslings' yellowish down gradually gives way to the dark plumage of their parents; the distinctive white cheek patch begins to show at six weeks. At two months they are nearly indistinguishable from the adults. By next spring, with their parents breeding again, the year-old goslings will be on their own.

Their new feathers are a marvel of insulation, quite warm enough for our coldest winters. The handsome, almost iridescent black feathers of the outer layer overlap to shed water. Underneath is a layer of soft, warm down. At this time of year, in midsummer, the outer feathers lie flat over the down. As autumn approaches, the goose's twelve thousand tiny skin muscles will flex to raise the feathers and increase the air space between them and the down, providing even more insulation.

Meanwhile the young geese's wings are growing powerful pinions with strong flight feathers at the edges. (American Indians used these tough feathers on their arrow shafts.) And during this same time their parents' wings become useless; a few weeks after their goslings have hatched, Canada geese molt. It is nearly a month before their new feathers have grown, by which time the goslings are ready to follow them into the air. In earlier years this molting period was a perilous time; but today, at least in our suburbs, most of the geese's large predators are gone.

And a Canada goose is rarely taken by surprise. Whenever I come upon them, it is obvious that they have seen me first. The Canada's eye can detect colors and is proportionately much larger than that of a beach-walker or almost any other mammal. Bulging beside each of its white cheeks, the eyes can take in a 250-degree range, compared to a maximum 180 degrees for a man. The goose's eyesight is extremely sharp, having evolved to scout a landing area from a high altitude during migration. Occasionally I've seen a goose on the ground suddenly glance up at what looked like an empty sky and give a honk or two; shortly a flock appeared like dots strung out overhead. The Canada goose's eye is also adapted to its aquatic life, with a semi-transparent nictitating membrane that evidently closes over the eye under water and protects it from windblown sand on land; it also keeps the eye clean and moist.

You can't see the Canada goose's ears, but they are there, and they work very well, detecting the slightest noise at an impressive distance. Apparently the Canada's sense of smell is even less developed than mine, which is just as well for the goose, considering the odorous mess it makes.

It is not difficult to tell where the local Canadas have been feeding. The grass is cropped as if a close-cutting lawnmower had just been through it. The goose's bill is a remarkable instrument, long and tapered, with sharp serrations along the side and a pair of curved choppers at the end. It is powerful enough to shovel sand and mud away to get at any food underneath. And with some two thousand tactile connections to nerve endings, the bill can select what grass or seeds the goose wants and reject the dross, even underwater. It also makes a formidable slashing weapon when the goose is cornered or defending its nest.

Unlike most water birds, our Canada geese seem to spend most of their time on land. If hungry enough, they will eat mussels or small crabs. And they gulp down a few pebbles for their gizzards. But when they can't get picnic sandwiches, they prefer a vegetarian diet. And while they forage on our lawns, golf courses, and beach grass, I sometimes wonder if, besides joining our picnics, they have also adopted some of our other social manifestations. Watching and listening to an occasional goose gathering, I'm re-

minded of a gaggle of Greenwich partygoers. The participants stand about, posing, jostling, and gabbling at one
another, some snorting, a few hissing, others squawking or
honking, most yuk-yukking, all creating a veritable din.

And like some of our partygoers, Canada geese spend
an inordinate amount of time preening—in their case literally. At first, watching them nip and prod and rub their
bills over their bodies, I mistakenly assumed that Canada
geese were badly infested with lice. They do have lice, but
they preen regularly for a more practical reason. Near the
goose's tail is its uropygial gland, which exudes a waxy oil
that the goose rubs off with its bill and smears onto its
feathers. Then it rubs its head on the oiled feathers. The
uropygial oil waterproofs and lubricates the feathers and
keeps the bill itself from drying and cracking. I have
watched a gaggle of geese go through their preening devot-
edly for nearly an hour, then go into the water for a wild
display of splashing. Rising out of the water, flapping their
wings, dipping their heads, sometimes turning completely
over, they wash off any sand that may have collected on
their oiled feathers.

In late autumn, when the winter visitors arrive, I can
see what different birds they are. They come in high and
honking, usually in a perfect V, their wingbeats deceptively
slow. Sometimes they circle for a closer inspection of the
cove. They have covered perhaps a thousand miles or more
at a cruising speed of forty miles an hour, all but the leader
(who changes frequently) using the V formation to ride the
wind wave of the bird ahead. They have been seen traveling
at great altitudes; aviators have sighted Canada geese as
high as nine thousand feet, flying at sixty-five miles an
hour. As they come in for a landing they throttle down to
thirty miles an hour or less. Unlike migrating swans, which
usually fly nonstop to their destination, the geese have

paused frequently for refreshment along the way. So they are in good shape, though not as fat as our local geese.

A Canada lands with aerodynamic expertise learned long before the airplane was invented. Skimming across the water, the goose lowers its wing feathers like flaps, sticks its tail down, extends its legs with webbed feet spread to take the impact, raises its wings to stall out, and hits the water with tail and feet in a perfect three-point landing. The geese make much the same landing on a beach or fairway, running a few steps forward until they lose momentum.

When ice forms on the inland ponds and lakes, more Canadas fly to our cove, where the salt water has not yet frozen; if it too begins to freeze, they paddle about breaking it up. With their well-insulated plumage, they are not bothered by the ice, and if snow comes to their feeding areas, they gather near the houses for handouts that are not long in coming. By spring, many of the visitors have reached the logical conclusion that migration is for the birds, and have joined our local geese.

So our Canada goose population expands yearly, abetted by a healthy birth rate—which nature originally predicated on mortal dangers that no longer exist. A Canada goose in our protected environment can live a dozen years or more. (Captive Canadas have made it to forty years.) I've seen some that appear positively patriarchal. And a pair produces some five offspring every one of their mated years. No wonder our town authorities feel confronted with goose gridlock. Various and wonderful have been the devices used by them to urge the geese to depart. But our town fathers have been no match for the stubborn intelligence of *Branta canadensis canadensis*.

On Greenwich's Byram Beach, which sometimes has more geese than human swimmers, the officials tried a "goose gooser," a foot-high, low-voltage electric fence. But they could not plug it in during daytime hours when the toddlers were there, a fact that the geese quickly discovered. The theory was that the geese were too fat to jump over it at night, and would leave the area once they were shocked by it. Watching the elaborate installation, a local fisherman commented, "The geese will outsmart them. They have every other time." They did this time too, simply flying over the fence. The only victim was one very shocked squirrel.

Byram Beach's caretakers then tried noisemakers. Firecrackers seemed only to amuse the geese. A signal cannon borrowed from a local yacht club was fired as the geese made their morning arrival at 8:00 A.M. The blast hardly caught their attention, but it woke up everybody in the neighborhood. One caretaker decided it was time for the "crackerscreamer," a formidable gun-fired shell that exploded over the geese with a bloodcurdling shriek. That did it—but again only temporarily.

An indication of local reaction to the infestation of the geese was the flood of suggestions to Town Hall—four thousand of them, nearly one idea for every goose in Greenwich. Not all were feasible. Bird dogs might have worked except for a long-standing ban on dogs at the beach; some people felt that dogs were more of an annoyance than geese. Importing hawks appeared impractical; hawk-shaped helium balloons were tried with no success. Vacationing students hired to run shouting across the beach bothered the sunbathers more than the geese (and proved too expensive). Fire hoses were equally unpopular, the geese being better waterproofed than the people.

The most intriguing deterrent was conceived by Patrick Lucas, superintendent of the local Innis Arden golf club, who had noted that swans defending their nests attacked all intruders, including geese. If the Canada goose was so smart, Lucas reasoned, the sight of a swan family on his golf course should warn the geese away. When I first heard of Lucas's proposition, I was doubtful because I have seen numerous swans and geese swimming alongside one another in our cove. But evidently the sight of those cygnets made the geese think twice, because Mr. Lucas's device worked at his golf club. It consisted of two adult swans and three cygnets, all made of polystyrene and set out on one of the water hazards.

Mr. Lucas even made up kits of his artificial swans and sold some to other golf-course superintendents. But not all of them worked. In nearby Westport the Canada geese proved smart enough to notice that the swans rarely moved, and promptly alighted alongside them. At some other golf courses the geese simply stayed away from the water hazards, fouling the fairways and greens even more.

Greenwich officials tried an ordinance banning the feeding of Canada geese. But the park-goers continued to feed the ducks, only to see the larger geese (which apparently had not read the ordinance) snap up most of the food. Even the U.S. Fish and Wildlife Service was enlisted; it obliged by rounding up hundreds of geese during their molting season, penning them in crates and flying them north—to the disgust of many taxpayers who ridiculed the cost of forty dollars per goose for critters too lazy to fly north themselves for their summer vacation. Besides, many of them returned as soon as they could fly again. (The town fathers knew because the geese had been banded.)

My hunting friends have what they consider a simple solution. But the Canada goose has been protected by the Migratory Bird Treaty Act since 1918. The law permits the Secretary of the Interior to allow some goose hunting, and it is a sign of Connecticut's urgent problem that it has the longest open season of any of the Eastern coastal states: ninety days. But it is estimated that to keep the geese at zero population growth would require killing half of them every year, a slaughter that would elicit an outcry from nature lovers.

The longer hunting season has increased the goose hunters' kill, but only by about 10 percent. The geese in the wild seem to outsmart the hunters nearly as much as they do our local officials. Some environmentalists claim that fewer geese are killed by guns than die from eating lead shot that has missed the target (and accordingly have advocated the substitution of such pellets). As far as Greenwich is concerned, another state law bans firearms within five hundred feet of any habitation (a fairly good definition of the suburbs). Our Canada geese appear to know that. And during the hunting season, some hunters maintain, the rural geese, evidently at the first sound of gunfire, take off for the suburbs, thereby expanding rather than curbing our local goose population.

Not surprisingly, the many goose-limiting proposals include birth control and abortion. New York's Bronx Zoo has tried to cope with its goose invasion by capturing some of the males and performing vasectomies; given our number of geese, it might be easier to diaper all of them. Some of my neighbors, more attracted to swans than to geese (no doubt because of the numbers), have reacted to the state's proposal to addle swan eggs by urging that they concentrate on goose eggs instead.

There remain some neighbors whose enjoyment of these stately birds outweighs the annoyance; some even argue that the geese nurture their lawns by close-cropping and fertilizing the grass. And there are those who would settle for milder measures to discourage the unwelcome visitors. Canada geese, they claim, prefer Kentucky blue-grass to red fescue grass, so why not plant the latter? The geese also prefer closely mown grass, some ornithologists maintain; if we let our lawns grow into meadows, the geese would go elsewhere. But not many suburbanites, who were attracted here by manicured lawns, are prepared for that step. Other goose experts say that Canadas like water views. "The real problem with geese," said one, "is that people have these big, lush lawns that go right down to the water. You could not construct a better Canada goose feeder if you tried." The geese tend to shun lawns where they cannot see the pond or cove for a quick getaway. So why not plant trees or bushes along the shore?

That may be one reason why I can still enjoy the geese—because they have not yet invaded my lawn. Clearly they regard it as inferior since its level is below that of the seawall, obscuring the goose's water view.

But you can't put a wall around a water hazard, nor can you surround it with bushes and trees. And noisemakers don't help on a golf course, particularly within earshot of the putting green. So most of our golf courses have their resident Canada geese. In fact, the Yale ornithologist Charles Sibley says that he is frequently called out to treat a Canada goose that has been beaned by a golf ball. Some golfers' opinion of the geese was voiced by Bobby Shipps, the greenskeeper of Norwalk's Shorehaven Golf Club, when informed that a ball had killed a goose. "Give that golfer a medal," said Mr. Shipps.

Goosewise, as the admen would say, I seem to have the best arrangement. The Canada geese don't bother me, and I can goggle at our local gaggles whenever I want to stroll along the beach (being careful where I step). Watching these imperious critters strut about their domain or honk in ragged flight formation from cove to pond, I can only marvel at this paradoxical example of learning over instinct. The Canada goose has managed to suppress the most fundamental avian urge, the one for which it is superbly designed: the urge to migrate.

FIVE

Deer in the Orchard

EVERYBODY around me is complaining about deer. They seem to be everywhere, devastating orchards, feasting on gardens, even invading downtown streets. One Greenwich couple reported watching nearly a hundred of them in a single group parading across a meadow. A 130-pound buck got his antlers tangled in a soccer net. Another deer kept trying to go through a local car wash. Still another dropped into a restaurant—literally by jumping through the glass door. Yet another wandered into a local dress store. (It was a doe; nothing queer about Greenwich's deer.) At Bridgeport's Remington Arms Company, a management meeting was interrupted by a deer trying to enter the con- ference room—which seems only fair, considering the numbers of deer killed by guns. A local newspaper colum- nist, Jerry Dumas, employing perhaps understandable hy- perbole, complained, "Where I live, you sometimes have to knock the deer out of the way with a rolled-up newspaper if you want to get the car out. . . . They think they own the place." Dumas claimed that on his property he had to wear boots to wade through the "foop," his word for deer-doo.

Environmentalists estimate that there are some 30,000 deer in Connecticut. That's more than at any time since the seventeenth century, and almost thirty thousand more than at the turn of this century. There are an estimated one thousand of them in Greenwich alone. While eating their way through the suburbs, they are also running into automobiles. A state conservation officer claims that his men are devoting most of their time to removing dead deer from the roads. "These are 150-pound animals," he complained. "We've had officers injure their backs and hips picking up deer."

Our problem is mirrored in almost every other American suburb. New York's Westchester County swarms with deer, whose population has nearly doubled in a decade. A state conservationist refers to this new breed as "yuppie deer who are used to people and find they can eat shrubbery near people's houses." A Westchester friend of mine, surveying his cropped garden, suggested only half in jest that the local nurserymen were bribing the deer with salt licks to create more business. The nurseries, however, are also victims, especially in the spring, when their young plants start to blossom. According to zoologist Michael Conover, a single deer can consume several hundred plants in one night.

On Fire Island, New York, early-morning joggers are ambushed by deer looking for handouts; one knocked a woman off her bicycle. When not frightening joggers, they are gobbling up prized flowers. "Lilies and tulips are like *crème brûlée* to them," says one Fire Island gardener. Another, who had lovingly planted fifty tulip bulbs, grumbled, "One day they were just about to open. The next day they were gone."

There are so many nearly tame deer on Long Island that they are endangering airport runways as well as highways. When realtor-publisher Mortimer Zuckerman's private plane smacked into one at the East Hampton airport, he asked permission to send his limousine down the runway to clear it whenever he was flying in; town officials denied permission, for some reason. In upstate New York, a deer walked into a Tarrytown butcher shop, presumably just looking. There are so many hungry deer in that part of the state that an orchard owner shot forty of them and still could not keep the rest from consuming 90 percent of his new trees.

New Jersey's deer population has also nearly doubled in the last decade. In Princeton the number rose from two hundred to more than one thousand in a decade. Hunterdon County has forty to fifty of them per square mile. "I've seen more deer than squirrels here," one woman claimed. They wander through gardens and onto patios, helping themselves to flowers and bird feeders and begging through the windows. A New Jersey suburbanite said, "What scares me is that they don't even get out of the way for traffic." A buck that crashed through the show window of a Princeton gift shop was one of a herd that regularly hangs out at a nearby parking lot. Others have been found paddling about in local swimming pools.

Pennsylvania's deer are consuming an estimated $16 million worth of flowers, fruit, and other growing things per year. Some of the deer have even moved from the suburbs into the cities; there are now more deer inside city limits than there were in the entire state in the nineteenth century. One Philadelphian reported watching a number of the critters standing at the traffic light at Ridge Avenue and Spring Lane. "I don't think they were waiting for the light to change," he said, but he wasn't sure. Richard L. James, executive director of Philadelphia's Schuylkill Center, an environmental-education park inside the city limits, says of the invading deer, "I do not consider them to be wildlife anymore. I push them out of the way to get to work."

Out in the Pennsylvania suburbs, one resident says she doesn't need an alarm clock; every morning at the same time she is awakened by the commuters' cars honking at the deer in the road. A neighbor adds, "They're like dogs— no fear at all . . . and each year it's worse."

Maryland's deer population tripled during the 1980s. At Camp David, the presidential retreat, they are more than a match for the Secret Service; the trees and shrubs are all bare below six feet, the height of a deer foraging on its hind legs. The nuns of a Baltimore County convent held some anguished discussions when a huge buck invaded the sacred grounds. For a while his protectors argued, "How can we kill this wonderful creation of God?" But when he started eating the yews surrounding the crucifix, a professional archer was called in. The buck weighed in at 250 pounds, and the nuns and the archer shared the venison. So many Maryland deer have been killed by cars—and so many cars have been wrecked—that the state has constructed "deer tunnels" under some of the highways. But so far most of the deer have continued to prefer the roads; evidently they can't, or don't bother to, read the signs. (New Jersey highway officials have tried to lure the deer onto overpasses lined with grass.)

Our Northeastern problem seems to have spread all the way west. In the affluent Hillsborough suburb of San Francisco, swarming with some six hundred deer, residents proposed emulating Maryland's nuns by hiring a deer-slayer. "A friend of mine's Porsche was wrecked recently by a deer," one man complained. A garden club member lamented, "For the past two years I could not leave my yard without closing a gate. Talk about being a prisoner."

Not surprisingly, the local humane society members demurred, one of them professing, "We believe that an animal's life is more valuable than a rose-bush." And the town's police chief had a pragmatic reaction: "The last thing I want to see is news headlines that say 'Hillsborough Cops Kill Bambi.' " At this writing the Hillsborough Bambis remain undisturbed.

So I'm told by my neighbors and the press. Our own gardens have been spared, probably because we do not have enough forest nearby for the deer's retreat. The last deer that went through our property ran across the lawn, nimbly jumped the seawall, and swam out to the nearest island in the cove. That was two decades ago; but my friends in the forested backcountry warn me that it is only a matter of time before population pressure, as the environmentalists call it, drives the deer down even into our more crowded habitat.

So once again I went looking for books and experts. And once again I found myself sympathizing with the alleged culprit. After all, how can you help but be fascinated by a critter that has four stomachs and a huge heart, defecates every two hours, doesn't sweat, walks on high heels, was once worshiped, and can leap seven feet straight into the air, run at forty miles an hour, swim at fifteen miles an hour, and even masturbate?

For one thing, the deer were here first. *Peterson's Field Guide to the Mammals* claims that deer fossils have been dated to the Oligocene period, some 30 million years ago. They have survived while animals like the saber-toothed tiger and the mastodon came and went. Today's North American deer are more native American than our Indians. By the Pleistocene period, as long as one million years ago, they had already consolidated into three species; we now call one of them the mule deer and another the blacktail, both of which are found west of the Mississippi; the third, which inhabits our eastern suburbs, is the whitetail.

There are some thirty subspecies of the whitetail in North America, as specialized as a Florida Keys deer and even a Hilton Head Island deer. But the one that most of us from New England and across the northern United States deal with is the whitetail. It stands about three and a half feet high at the shoulders, weighs 150 to two hundred pounds and has a scientific Latin name that is a typographical error.

A Franco-German scientist named Constantine Samuel Rafinesque, who had settled in the United States, came upon a fossil of a whitetail deer tooth in a Virginia cave in 1832 and decided to classify its genus with the Latin name for "concave tooth." Evidently his zoology was better than his Latin, because the name he chose was *Odocoileus*, instead of the correct word, *Odontocoileus*; the former name, added to *virginianus* because of the site where the fossil was found, became the accepted taxonomic term for our whitetail, misspelling included, plus a third Latin name, *borealis*, to identify the northern whitetail.

Naming the whitetail (sometimes given as white-tailed) deer for its teeth was significant, because it does have a peculiar mouth. At the rear of its jaw are normal concave molars for chewing. But the whitetail has no incisors, or biting teeth, at the front of its upper jaw. A browsing deer grabs a bud or tree branch by chomping its lower incisors against a rough, padded gum on the roof of its jaw, ripping the food away instead of biting it off. You can tell whether a deer or a rabbit, for example, has been enjoying your garden by studying the damage. If the tulips or carrot tops have been nipped off neatly, it was a rabbit; if they were yanked off, it was a deer.

Not only were there deer in North America long before suburbanites; they were almost essential to Native Americans and European settlers alike. What the bison was to the Plains Indians, the deer was to the Eastern Indians of the forest. On a given day, one of these early Americans could be found sitting in front of his lodge, clothed in deerskin pants, shirt, and vest, his deerskin leggings tied with deer sinew and his deerskin moccasins stuffed with insulating deer hair as he worked with tools made of deer bone to fashion weapons or ornaments from deer antlers and hooves. Nearby his wife prepared their dinner of venison or bone marrow. So vital was the deer to the mound-building Indians of Ohio that they worshiped the animal, and wore, for ceremonial purposes, sacred headdresses made of antlers.

The earliest immigrants quickly learned the many uses of the deer. They made candles and soap from deer tallow, used strips of buckskin for snowshoes and antlers for hat and gun racks, carved deer bones into knife and pistol handles, and stuffed their furniture with deer hair. A brisk transatlantic trade in deerskins and venison sustained thousands of settlers who became professional deerslayers. In his classic book *The Deer of North America*, Leonard Lee Rue III reports on one of these hunters, Mishack Browning, who slew nearly two thousand whitetails during a forty-four-year career. Some 2 million pounds of deerskins went off to England from Savannah, Georgia, alone in the period from 1755 to 1773.

At the time, there appeared to be plenty of deer for everybody. Ernest Thompson Seton estimated that in the early nineteenth century there were 40 million whitetails in the United States (Rue thinks this figure is about a hundred percent too high). But in succeeding years so many were slaughtered that the whitetail was threatened with extinction. By the time hunting restrictions were finally imposed, there were fewer than two hundred deer in New Jersey, and a deer sighting in New England merited a page-one story in the local paper. What saved the whitetail was a series of antihunting laws stricter than those we have today. Then came tree-cutting and suburban development, and the whitetail's population rebound was under way. Current estimates vary widely, but there are probably 20 million whitetails in the United States now.

If, as many gardeners protest, that is too many deer, it's largely our fault. As we spread out from the cities, felling the forest and raising condos, we gave little thought to wildlife except to assume that it would go away. What we didn't realize was that the whitetail deer was an especially adaptable animal. There are more deer today in suburban Fairfield County than in rural Connecticut. A friend who has homes in Fairfield County and Vermont discovered that hunters in the latter state were complaining about a lack of deer; meanwhile his New Canaan, Connecticut, yard swarms with them. New Jersey's Raritan and Hunterdon counties have more deer per square mile than New York's wild Adirondacks.

The deer's best habitat is what zoologists call an "edge," an area of open field or swamp where deer can feed, bordering a forest where they can hide. That is exactly what we have been providing for them as we cut back the forests. The whitetail likes this habitat because it is suited to its four stomachs—or, technically, the four chambers of its digestive system. A member of the order Artiodactyla, the deer belongs to the suborder Ruminantia, or ruminants, animals that chew cuds. Domestic ruminants include cows, sheep, and goats, but the earlier ruminants evolved over some 30 million years as a natural defense against predators.

The ruminant's motto is "bite now, chew later." It grazes in the open, where the choicest food is found, but does not stop to eat it there.

As it chomps away at buds and grasses, facing into the wind so its superb sense of smell can detect danger, the deer keeps moving to stay ahead of any predators that may be stalking it from behind. It swallows its food almost whole into the first food compartment, the rumen. In a good field of grass it can fill its rumen with eight quarts in a couple of hours. Then it retires to the safety of the woods or a refuge with a good vantage point, where it can settle down and eat in peace.

Meanwhile, those buds and grasses have soaked and fermented in the rumen, making them more digestible. The deer calls back this food in globules, or cuds, about the size of a crabapple, which it masticates thoroughly with a side-to-side motion of its jaw, its efficient molars grinding twigs, acorns, and even cherry pits into pulp. During the process it usually keeps its head up and its senses on watch, dozing only from time to time. After some forty chews it swallows the cud and brings up another.

The masticated food bypasses the deer's rumen and goes into the second stomach, the reticulum, which has a honeycombed lining, and whose chief function is to detect and reject any harmful objects. Deer reticulums have been found to contain bits of stone and glass; one had a cartridge case.

Well chewed and filtered, the food now passes to the third compartment, the omasum, and the fourth, the abomasum, where it is finally digested. The whole process can take twenty or more hours before the nutrients pass into the deer's sixty-five feet of intestine to be absorbed into the bloodstream; the undigested leftovers become pellets for excretion. Deer pellets, as many as three hundred in a pile, resemble those of a rabbit, except that they are elongated rather than round. By this time the deer has gone back to grazing again; a grown whitetail will consume about six pounds of food a day.

If interrupted, the whitetail can respond almost with the speed of lightning. Its hair-trigger senses can detect the slightest danger. The deer's eyes are essentially color-blind; a hunter's red cap registers as a shade of gray. I recall coming upon some deerstalkers in a nearby forest and wondered at their camouflage; it made no difference to the deer, but made them more tempting to other hunters.

The whitetail's eyes bulge a quarter of an inch above its skull, giving it some 300 degrees of vision, about 50 percent of it binocular. It has excellent night vision. Although its eyes cannot sharply outline what they see, they can spot the slightest movement. If you come upon a deer and stand perfectly still, it probably won't be able to make you out. But the merest twitch of an arm or even the blink of an eye will set it off on the run.

The chance of such a confrontation is small because of the deer's other senses. If the wind and humidity are right, it can smell danger half a mile away. (Hunters should not eat garlic; indeed, some plaster themselves with "buck-lure" perfumes). And the whitetail's large ears, which can rotate almost like radar dishes, will pick up the faintest sound nearly as far away. Most deer also learn which sounds are threatening and which are not. Whitetails are smart enough to know that the best grass grows along highways, fertilized by the transportation department, warmed by sun-absorbing concrete or macadam, and watered copiously by cars splashing rain. They quickly learn that autos are no threat, and they rarely lift their heads at the roar of traffic—yet they never learn to stay off the highway itself.

Deer have been seen browsing in military reservations, oblivious to the blast of heavy artillery. And there have been instances of deer being attracted by the noise of a chain saw, evidently aware that the sound promises fallen trees with fresh leaves. But the snap of a twig underfoot or the alarm call of a bird provides an instant alert. I remember once scaring up a grouse, whose noisy flurry was immediately followed by an escaping deer I had not seen hiding in the brush.

When alarmed, the whitetail will usually stomp the ground and give a loud snort to warn other deer and immediately take off. It runs on the cloven hooves of what is called the Cervidae family. The deer's hoof is small, split in two, and sharp. A whitetail doe appears to be walking on high heels, delicately picking her way through the underbrush. Most bucks, however, scarcely lift their feet as they slog along. In a few inches of snow you can easily distinguish a doe's dainty tracks from the grooves made by the buck dragging his feet.

But both buck and doe use the excellent traction of their sharp hooves to dash away at forty miles an hour, leaping high in the air in great, ground-gulping strides. They seem almost to fly, covering twenty feet or more in a jump; some zoologists say they do it to get a better view of what lies ahead. With the same bounding lope they can cruise along for miles at thirty to thirty-five miles an hour. There is one report of a running deer clearing a seven-and-a-half-foot-high obstacle in a twenty-nine-foot jump; it was, however, going downhill. The whitetail's heart is about twice the size of a human's; on the run it pumps blood through its arteries at about 180 beats per minute, double that of man. In contrast, the heart of a relaxed, cud-chewing deer beats only forty times a minute.

A running buck may or may not raise his tail to expose

its white underside; a running doe always does. The twitching white tail and the exposed white rump serve as danger signals to the other deer in the area, who usually follow. The white tail is, of course, what gives this species of deer its name; in some areas it is called a bannertail.

It is also an excellent swimmer. Deer use ponds or lakes to escape from insects or predators, or simply to cool off. Some does will swim out to an island to give birth in a protected spot. One whitetail was sighted five miles off Cape Cod. A fisherman clocked another swimming at thirteen miles an hour in a burst of speed before settling down to a steady ten miles an hour. Others have been seen swimming at fifteen miles an hour.

Unlike many other mammals, the whitetail is nonterritorial; it does not select and mark its boundaries and defend its territory from intruders. The ideal habitat of meadow, swamp, and new-growth trees, bordered by a protecting forest, will attract herds of whitetails, who rarely wander more than four hundred yards away from the protective forest so long as there is enough food. Usually they travel in groups that are normally single-parent, matriarchal families, with one doe leading a couple of fawns plus two or three older yearlings. The fawns may include a young buck or two. But after a couple of years the bucks generally go off on their own. What some hunters or hikers mistake for a deer family with father and mother is instead a single mother with a yearling son sprouting his first antlers. Soon he will be wandering about in lonely splendor, ignoring his mother and sisters until the autumnal surge of testosterone in his system signals the mating season. Then he goes crazy.

Through spring and summer the buck's antlers have been sprouting, covered with a velvety skin and nourished by blood vessels as they grow at about a quarter of an inch a day. By October the skin is peeling and hanging in tatters.

The blood supply shuts off and the antlers harden. Unlike sheep, which have permanent horns, the buck deer grows a new set of antlers every year. Most have about eight points, though some well-fed bucks may grow huge antlers with more than eighteen points. Antlers serve as a secondary sex characteristic, identifying the buck to the color-blind doe just as the peacock's feathery finery attracts the color-sensitive peahen. In fact, zoologists have found in experiments that when a buck's antlers are cut off, he loses interest in breeding. When others injected testosterone into two does, it stimulated them to grow antlers about eight inches long.

By mid-October the buck is "in rut." His testes have enlarged and descended. His appetite for food, his usual mild disposition, even his natural caution are forgotten in his preoccupation with sex. For a month or more he is frustrated because the whitetail doe normally does not reach estrus, her day—and it is usually no more than a day—of sexual willingness, until mid-November. A particularly pent-up buck may temporarily relieve his passion with masturbation, humping his back and rubbing his ten-inch penis against his belly. But most of the buck's waking hours are spent running about, nose down, grunting every few steps as he searches for the trail of a doe.

At this point he is in his prime. A whitetail buck usually gains his full weight of up to 150 pounds by October, again a month before the doe. In the process of rubbing his antlers against trees to get rid of the peeling velvet, he has strengthened his neck, which is also swollen by the testosterone in his system. Now, however, in his single-minded search for a mate, he begins to lose weight.

After what must seem an eternity, he picks up a promising scent. A doe about to reach estrus emits a teasing odor for a couple of weeks before she is ready. And when a buck following the lure locates her, he often finds a couple of others already on the scene and ready to do battle for her favors. The moment of confrontation has come. The buck, you might say, stops here.

Actually, the confrontation between two whitetail bucks is usually more a mock battle than a deadly conflict. Two contending males, hair on end, face each other with what some zoologists call the "hard look." Each gives the other an opportunity to study the size of his antlers. Frequently that is enough; the buck with the larger antlers becomes the dominant male and the other backs off. But if he does not, they move closer, grunting, snorting, pawing the ground, and circling each other in a slow, stiff-legged dance until one lunges at the other.

Sometimes this is enough to make one of them retreat. If not, they continue to bang their antlers together in a clicking, thudding minuet that usually lasts for only a few minutes before one decides he has been bettered. On rare occasions they lock antlers; if they do, and are unable to disengage, they are doomed to a lingering death, unable to move about to eat. Whitetail corpses have been found with their antlers still locked together. When the first one dies, it drags the survivor to the ground to expire. Deer expert Leonard Rue III reports discovering two such victims, one still alive, the other half-eaten by marauding dogs. On one occasion, three entangled buck carcasses were found, indicating a battle in which a third buck joined the fight and succeeded only in locking all three sets of antlers in a deadly embrace.

In most encounters, the defeated buck goes off in search of another doe; sometimes, though, he will merely retire to a safe distance. The doe meanwhile pays little attention to these macho goings-on. And if she is not yet ready when the dominant buck approaches her, she clamps her tail down and dashes away—the only time a doe runs without lifting her white tail.

If, however, she is ready, she stands still while he licks her about the head, and responds by licking him and rubbing her body against his. Whitetail deer have no concept of incest; she may be the buck's sister, mother, or even daughter or granddaughter. She braces herself as he mounts her, and the force of his half-minute of thrusting can drive her to her knees.

A whitetail doe's estrus may last only a day, but she makes the most of it. They stay together, mating as many as a couple dozen times before she loses interest and wanders away. Occasionally during the day she will accept a defeated buck while the dominant male is recovering from his last mating. By the second day the doe usually refuses all advances, and the bucks go off in search of others.

During this short period in November, there are plenty of does looking for mates. (A deer hunter's saying I recall hearing as a youngster was that for every buck looking to make some doe, there are a couple of does looking to make a buck.) And the whitetail buck's principle seems to be to leave no doe unmounted. So, during this brief, busy time, one buck may fertilize some twenty does.

By the end of November his pituitary gland, responding to decreasing sunlight, signals the end of the rutting season. His testosterone level subsides. His neck resumes its normal size. And his antlers fall off, decomposing on the forest floor to provide calcium and other nutrients for the smaller animals.

The buck's hormones have done their part in preserving the species. But he is some twenty-five pounds underweight. His immediate need is to preserve himself by gaining weight for the hard days and nights ahead—if, that is, he has not already provided too easy a target for hunters while heedlessly pursuing a mate. Fall and winter are the most dangerous time of year for the whitetail buck; if he escapes the hunter but does not regain his fat, he still may not survive.

By late autumn, both buck and doe have grown their winter coats, a dense mass of darker hair, often called the "blue coat" as opposed to the summer "red coat." The winter hair is long and hollow, the air inside providing extra insulation. (A swimming deer rides higher in the water in winter than summer.) Beneath the outer coat appears an inner lining as soft as cashmere, providing the same kind of insulation as our winter "thermal" underwear. This combination of outer and inner coat becomes so long and thick as the winter progresses that if the temperature goes above forty degrees Fahrenheit, the deer has to find shade to cool off.

By late autumn its food has changed from summer grasses to seasonal apples and acorns. With its keen sense of smell, a whitetail can detect an apple orchard half a mile away. They feast on the fruit so greedily that when a storm litters the ground with windfalls, the deer often get what is called "rumen overload," a bloated backup from the first stomach. The deer also clean the ground of acorns, and have been known to wait under oak trees for acorns that the squirrels drop to the ground.

Whitetails also eat falling leaves, especially dogwood and maple, and have learned to select the newly fallen because of the moisture they still retain. Though color-blind, the deer can pick out by smell the red leaves, which have a higher sugar content. They gobble up fallen leaves at the rate of nearly forty a minute; a two-hundred-pound deer can consume nearly ten thousand leaves in a day.

The deer fatten up, but do not hibernate. Neither do they migrate, though some may travel short distances to

safer, more sheltered winter locations. With snow in the air and winds growing colder, they "yard up" in a low area protected from the wind by evergreens, which make a better roof against the snow than the bare branches of deciduous trees. The snow depth on the ground in such areas may be half that in the open. The black tree trunks absorb whatever heat there is from the winter sun, and the temperature in the yard may be twenty degrees warmer than in the open. The does, leading their fawns and year-lings, often return to the same yard each winter. Soon they are joined by bands of bucks, their antlers and sex urge gone, and the herd settles in for the winter.

In mild weather they use the yard as a base, fanning out to feed on suburbanites' orchards and whatever remains of their gardens, and returning to ruminate and sleep. When the snow comes, they hunker down, curl up, and doze, waiting out the storm even if it lasts for days. Their heavily insulated winter coat provides such thermal protection that the snow does not melt on their backs. This is when the whitetail comes closest to hibernation, its metabolism idling while it waits. When the sky finally clears, the deer go out to feed again, trying to keep in the lee of the forest, out of the direct blast of the winter winds. When they can find it, they favor a sloping field facing south or west, where the sun has melted more of the snow. But when the snow is heavy and the gardens and windfall apples are covered, they reach for the branches above them, chomping at twigs for the little nourishment they provide.

Severe winter is a time for survival of the fittest within the herd and even within the family. The largest deer, able to reach the highest, get the major share of the tree branches. Driven by hunger, a doe may challenge a heavier buck, rising on her hind legs and slashing at him with her sharp front hooves. Some does even take food away from their own fawns, many of which do not survive the winter.

Their pointed hooves help them break pond ice to get at the water, and to dig through thin layers of snow for acorns and roots. But the hooves also give them very poor traction on ice; sometimes one will fall and skid about when it tries to scramble to its feet. The pointed toes also break through most snow crusts; only the heaviest incrustation permits them to reach higher into the trees for more twigs. The winter forest shows where the deer have been, with the tree branches chewed off to the height of the tallest whitetail.

But twigs and roots offer little nourishment and the

deer often expend more energy finding their food, gradually losing weight as the winter wears on. A doe weighing
130 pounds in autumn may shrink to one hundred pounds
during the winter. Many lose even more, and slowly starve.
A healthy adult whitetail can last about two months without food; a fawn will die after a month. A dying doe's
shoulders and legs begin to shake. Her hair stands on end
to increase insulation. She staggers, then stands still, with
her back to the wind. Finally she slumps to the ground and
quietly waits for death. The others around her pay no
attention, except for her fawn. It will try to nurse, then
approach another doe and be driven off until it too staggers,
falls, and dies. The University of California's A. Starker
Leopold estimates that in a harsh winter 2 million U.S.
whitetails starve to death.

With spring comes regeneration. At the first snow
melt, the deer leave the yard. Behind them lie the decomposing carcasses already fertilizing the forest floor. For the
survivors there are green buds and leaves of bushes and
trees, sprouting blades of succulent grasses and the promise
of suburban gardens. The deer are scrawny, and their winter coats are peeling off in patches. They are hungrier than
they have been all year, but instinctively they know enough
to eat sparingly at first.

Nearly all the does are eating for two. The fetus that
has developed slowly during the fasting winter now grows
quickly. By early May, after some 150 days of gestation,
the unborn fawn is about a foot long, weighs nearly five
pounds, already has its spotted coat, and is stirring in the
womb. Its sharp hooves are covered with a gelatinous goo
to protect the placental sac. The fetus will gain about another pound and add a few more inches by birth time.

The doe, puzzled by the movement inside her, starts
behaving strangely. For the only time during the year, she

becomes territorial, going off on her own, driving away intruders and even her yearlings. At first the anxious youngsters try to follow her, but after a few rebuffs they give up and wander about aimlessly, without the protective guidance to which they have been accustomed. More young deer are killed on the highway in May than in any other month.

One day in mid- to late May, the pregnant doe stops in her tracks, turns in circles, lies down, gets up, circles again, lies down again, and looks back as two small hooves appear. Within minutes her fawn lies beside her. A new-born doe weighs about five pounds, a buck about a pound more. Instinctively she licks it and eats the placenta so it will not be discovered by a predator. For the same reason, nature has provided the newborn with no body odor for its first few days. If this is the doe's firstborn, it is the only one. If the doe has had a fawn the previous year, it will probably have twins this time; next year it may well have triplets.

Slightly more than half of a whitetail's fawns are male (about 106 males for every 100 females). As with most mammals, the male is the weaker sex; this is nature's way of preserving the species. A whitetail buck will leave his mother sooner; he will be less resistant to disease; because of his preoccupation during the rutting season and his ant-lers' attraction to hunters, the buck will have a higher mortality rate.

The nursing milk of a whitetail has about twice as much butterfat as that of a Jersey cow, and the fawn gains 10 percent of its birth weight each day for the first week. Then the doe's butterfat content starts to drop and the fawn grows at the rate of about 5 percent per week. During most of these first few weeks the fawn lies concealed in the forest, its spotted coat providing perfect camouflage, resembling sunlight filtered through the leaves. If the doe has more than one fawn, she hides them separately. And if they remain still, they are almost impossible to detect, especially during the first odorless days; a dog sniffing through the forest will go right past them if they are well hidden. To further protect their hiding place, the mother generally keeps away from them except during feeding time. As a result, our state's Department of Environmental Protection gets frequent phone calls from people who have "rescued" what they assume to be an orphaned fawn. This can be a deadly mistake, since once the fawn is tainted by the scent of a human, its mother will abandon it.

Within a couple of weeks the fawn starts to roam about its hiding place while its mother is away. When she returns, she noses about for her infant, emitting a soft murmur that the fawn recognizes and responds to. At the slightest sign of a predator, she paces about, sniffing the air and clucking apprehensively. She will defend her fawns fiercely, lashing out with her sharp front feet. By now she can find the fawn by scent, because she has been teaching it an essential lesson of deer childhood: to pee on its legs.

The whitetail deer does not sweat; like a dog, it pants when hot. But each deer has its characteristic scent, permitting the members of a herd to recognize and follow one another. Some of this scent is exuded from glands between the deer's toes. But it also has two white tarsal glands on the inside of its hind legs; and the mother teaches each fawn how to urinate its special scent onto them and rub its legs together to preserve the odor so it will leave a trail. A ten-day-old fawn found staggering about in the underbrush is not still learning to walk; it is trying to keep its balance while rubbing its urine-stained legs together. Once the fawns start leaving their scent, a doe can pick out her own from the others, scarcely ever making a mistake.

The camouflage of the fawn, its spotted coat, is super-ficial. The white marks are at the hair tips, with the natural reddish brown beneath, rather like bleached blond hair on a human head. By summer the fawn's hair has grown, the white ends have worn off, and the fawn resembles a smaller version of a grown deer.

It is weaned gradually. As the doe's milk supply dwindles, she breaks off nursing after only a few minutes. If the hungry fawn persists, she butts it away. And if it is stubborn, she may even knock it over and hold it down with one of her feet. Within a month the fawn weighs nearly forty pounds and is finally learning to forage on grass; by this time its four ruminant stomachs are functioning. But not until October will it have a complete set of teeth.

The fawn also has the example of its sisters to follow. They have rejoined their mother, but their brothers have gone off with the other bachelors. The only bucks in the family now are the newly born. Their antlers will begin to sprout in April. Some of these young bucks may be sexually precocious and come into rut the first fall, when they are only a few months old. One of them may even try to mount his mother, to which she usually responds with an attack with those sharp front feet. Sometimes this rebuff fails to dampen his ardor, and he turns to one of his sisters.

If he or a passing buck impregnates a fawn, she will bring her single offspring with her when she rejoins her mother, now a grandmother at two and a half years. The matriarchal group, with the fawns about two-thirds the size of the mother, goes about the meadows, orchards, and gardens, retreating to the forest at night, through the late spring and summer, separated from the bucks until the autumn rutting season, and through the winter yarding until the pregnant does go off to give birth. When, after a few generations, the family group becomes too large, it will break up into new groups, each led by one of the dominant does.

Nearly 99 percent of all whitetail does conceive every year. In human terms it is as if all the young women in the neighborhood were pregnant, most of them with twins. Some zoologists have considered trying to shoot does with darts containing birth-control vaccine. But others argue that the cost—from forty-five dollars to three hundred dollars per doe—could be prohibitive, especially since about 80 percent of the does would have to be vaccinated. The doe's fertility was nature's way of compensating for the fact that the deer had so many predators. But man has interfered. The wolf, bear, lynx, and coyote, not as adaptable as the deer, have been crowded out of the suburbs.

A sign that the coyote may be making a comeback was reported by a friend whose Wilton, Connecticut, property has so many deer that they apparently have persuaded the coyotes to forget their natural shyness; he has even seen a couple of pups, indicating that a family has settled in. Another friend, in New Canaan, reported watching a large coyote pacing across his lawn; it was fat and sleek, further indicating a healthy supply of nutritious deer in the area. A Greenwich environmentalist says that there are coyotes lurking in our town, too, and points to the fact that several have been killed on the Merritt Parkway, which runs through the back country. Zoologists at Yale and Harvard claim that there is a new subspecies weighing about fifty pounds, which they call the eastern coyote, establishing itself in the Northeastern suburbs because, as Willie Sutton might have said if he'd been a coyote, that's where the venison is. The deer apparently have attracted coyotes to California, too, where suburbanites are complaining they are also snapping up wandering dogs and cats.

The whitetail deer also attracts many parasites. The nose botfly lays its eggs around the deer's nostrils; a snorting, coughing deer is trying to eject them. Deerflies are so named because they favor whitetails, which are also pestered by black flies, midges, and mosquitoes. Frequently during fly season, a herd of deer can be seen feeding in water up to their shoulders, just to get away from the clouds of insects. Assorted parasitical worms assault the whitetail's brain, eyes, throat, muscles, bladder, colon, and feet; they torment their host but are rarely lethal. And of course there is the now-famous deer tick, whose spirochete causes babesiosis and Lyme disease, prompting many humans to blame the population growth of the whitetail for the increase of these diseases (though the same ticks are carried by raccoons, skunks, squirrels, rabbits, field mice, and birds).

The deer's remaining major enemy is man. We kill hundreds of thousands of them just by automobile, nearly thirty thousand in Pennsylvania, for example, in one year. Road kills of deer in New York State have nearly doubled since 1980. One auto-safety expert calculated that in some states highway collisions alone reduce the deer population by as much as 20 percent—and enrich auto-body shops to the tune of more than $100 million a year. Our pet dogs, running in packs and reverting to a wild state, kill thousands more whitetails; dogs are particularly effective deer-slayers in the winter on lightly crusted snow that will carry their weight while the heavier, sharp-hoofed deer break through and flounder in the drifts. Snowmobiles can panic deer out of the protection of their winter yards. And human hunters cull the herds by more thousands.

Hunting, however, seems not to curb the whitetail population as much as many people think. Legally it is restricted and seasonal. Many states have "bucks only" laws, and even in states that permit both sexes to be shot, most hunters prefer the trophy of the antlered buck to the smaller doe, which meanwhile is reproducing itself exponentially. Not to mention what deer hunters call "the Bambi factor." A friend who occasionally hunts tells me that he doesn't dare come home to his wife and children with a dead doe; a buck, he says with a shrug, doesn't seem to bother them.

And there are the deer-lovers who feed them, as well as the hunter-haters, many of whom understandably fear for their own lives. Every autumn, deer hunters kill one another and innocent bystanders, the most famous recent incident being that of thirty-seven-year-old Karen Wood, in a suburb of Bangor, Maine, a mother of twins who was killed in 1988 while hanging out her laundry because she was wearing white mittens that a hunter mistook for a white tail. In Connecticut a jogger in a blue running suit was killed by a deer hunter. In Westchester a young man shot his mother when he mistook her for a deer. These incidents occur partly because so many hunters carelessly blast away at anything they see. Last year two hunters in their truck were so eagerly watching for deer on both sides of the road that they ran into one in front of them.

Many hunters, because of cold weather or conviviality, drink too much. A friend who lives in a Georgia suburb tells the story of three men who killed a deer and lost it off their truck bed three times before one of them realized that they hadn't put up the tailgate. In my state there are heavy penalties for drunken driving, but none for drunken hunting.

In the first twenty-four hours of New York's 1992 hunting season, three hunters were killed and four more were wounded. Some hunters who shoot people wind up in prison. One who killed a man in Connecticut got six years, but by strange bureaucratic logic the incident was not registered as a hunting death; because the hunter did not have a license and was using illegal ammunition, it was instead listed as "criminal activity." Many more hunting deaths are ruled accidents. One of Connecticut's Pequonnock Valley residents who has campaigned against deer hunting in the suburbs offers a modern argument: "I have spent my whole life here in this valley, and so did my father and his father. Our family hunted here for our food. But this is a different kind of place than it was even twenty years ago."

After a Greenwich couple found a dead deer near their patio, accosted a deer hunter on their property, and lost one dog and had another wounded, they spearheaded an anti-hunting pressure group that was joined by more than a thousand fellow suburbanites. Their goal is to ban hunting inside the town limits, arguing that rifles that can kill three miles away shouldn't be permitted in four-acre neighborhoods. State hunting laws that apply equally to rural and residential property, they complain, are like applying a fifty-five miles per hour highway speed limit to downtown Main Street. Connecticut statutes do not allow each town to have its own hunting laws. Whenever state legislators try to restrict hunting, they are overwhelmed by pro-gun lobbyists, although only 2.7 percent of the state's population are hunters.

Some animal-rights advocates march through the countryside making noise to scare the deer away from the hunters. Indeed, many of these campaigns have been so successful that in 1985 the hunters' lobbyists persuaded the Connecticut legislators to pass a law forbidding harassment of hunters. One Greenwich resident made an intriguing proposal in our local newspaper: limit the deer hunter's weapons to the lance and the club. Others argue that many state wildlife commissions encourage deer population growth to satisfy hunters whose permits pay their salaries. The number of hunting licenses sold each year in Connecticut has increased by 10 percent in the last decade. Wisconsin took in more than $17 million in license fees in 1983; and the state has more deer than it had 150 years ago.

Fewer people are killed in areas where deer hunting is restricted to bows and arrows. But besides maiming more deer than they kill—my Greenwich neighbors have reported seeing deer in their yards with arrows protruding from their flanks—the bow and arrow scares some suburbanites even more than the rifle. One study indicated that thirteen arrows are shot for each deer killed. And children playing in their yards cut their feet open on the razor-sharp blades of arrows that missed. A Westchester mother told me that during the hunting season she has to keep her children indoors for fear that they will get an arrow in the back. "I suddenly realized," she said, "that it was like the days when my great-great-grandmother had to keep the kids indoors because of the Indians. *Plus ça change. . . .*"

Although some twelve thousand deer are killed every year by hunters in Connecticut, about as many die of old age and starvation. And twice as many fawns do not make it through the first winter. A deer coddled in captivity can live fifteen years or more before its teeth are ground down. But few in the wild survive more than eight years. Because of his prized antlers, the life expectancy of a buck is about three and a half years. Those deer that make it through the perilous early years become wary and wise. A veteran buck will remain hidden during daylight hours unless flushed out. He naps with his nose pointed upwind, alert for any intrusion even when asleep. When on the move, he knows how to freeze at the approach of man, hidden by his natural camouflage. Frequently he will then circle back behind the hunter and keep him in view, ready to escape at a second's warning. Older does are just as canny. One, tagged as a fawn, survived for twenty-three years before finally being shot in 1983.

In some neighborhoods, the environmental officials have tried capturing deer and transporting them to wilder areas. But it is a sign of how much the deer have adapted to suburban living that when California wildlife officials rounded up twenty-nine of them in an area near San Francisco and trucked them to a wild deer refuge, all of them died within a few months. (The officials knew because of implanted radio devices.) Spoiled by the suburbanites, the deer were unable to cope with the harsh realities of the wild.

So the deer continue to eat my neighbors' apples and peaches and destroy the trees in winter by eating their bark. They lay waste to flower and vegetable gardens. (They particularly like strawberries.) Since they are mainly nocturnal feeders, it is difficult to catch them at it and drive them away. And many are so nearly tame that they saunter off for only a few yards, waiting to return when the coast is clear. Some suburbanites claim that the deer have excellent memories, returning frequently to the same opening in a fence. Environmentalists have calculated that deer consume more than 600 million tree seedlings every year. With human developers leveling about a million acres of trees a year, the deer see to it that they never grow tall again. In what seems to me a delicious irony, one Westchester developer is marketing a condominium settlement called Deer Valley, advertising it with a photograph of three deer crossing a meadow—probably on their way to somebody's garden.

But we can hardly blame the deer, since we are the ones who have provided the perfect habitat. And after learning more about these wild, graceful, adaptable, swift, intelligent, beautiful creatures, I tend to agree with my daughter, who enjoys her Westchester garden but considers the deer who invade it equally attractive. And, she says, "I'd rather not fence in my garden; somehow it would no longer seem like a country garden."

As she and other deer fanciers point out, there are some strategies for peaceful coexistence. One of the best is spelled out in *Gardening in Deer Country* by Karen Jescavage-Bernard, who wrote, "I didn't come to the country to fight nature." Her book lists hundreds of flowers, vegetables, bushes, and trees that deer find distasteful. For a few examples, most deer dislike boxwood, bayberry, lilac, jasmine, azalea, rosa rugosa, rhododendron, chinaberry, persimmon, holly, black locust, wax myrtle, narcissus, daffodil, jonquil, clematis, iris, lantana, asparagus, as well as tomatoes, onions, chives, mustard greens, kale, yarrow, foxglove, English ivy, and black pine. Many nurseries now label plants and shrubs according to deer preference. My daughter discovered that although her deer like geraniums, lilies, and roses, they keep away from marigolds, herbs, impatiens, and alyssum. They enjoy tulips of any color but yellow, which they avoid even in the bud, evidently by taste. She is content to have only yellow tulips. (Whitetails can also distinguish, evidently by smell, between poisonous and nonpoisonous mushrooms.)

Some gardeners and orchard owners, after pruning, pile the cuttings of plants deer dislike at the edges of the orchard and garden, as if to suggest that there's nothing here they'd like. They protect their trees from being debarked by covering the trunks with torn bedsheets. There are dozens of sprays that offend the deer's delicate sense of smell, though most of them are expensive and wash away in a rainstorm. A Westchester friend has her own recipe: one tablespoon of Tabasco sauce in a gallon of water; so far it has deterred her deer, but she too has to respray after a heavy rain. Some ecologists recommend sprays of wild animal (especially wolverine) urine; it isn't on everybody's shelf, but some nurseries and hardware stores stock it. Human urine seems to work as well and, of course, is more easily applied—if the neighbors don't object to the spectacle. A friend in a San Francisco suburb reports that a local nursery recommended packets of blood meal; the only problem was that her dogs gobbled them up. Others point out that the deer's keen sense of smell is offended by soap and human or dog hair, which can be scattered amidst the garden mulch. Some deer victims recommend hanging hair in pantyhose on the shrubs. But like sheets on the tree trunks, hedges swathed with bulging pantyhose tend to defeat the aesthetic purpose of landscaping.

Fencing tilted outward usually baffles the deer; they can jump over a straight fence up to seven feet high, but are confused by a tilted barrier. A Greenwich friend uses a device that emits a sound inaudible to human ears but annoying to a whitetail, an outdoor version of the sound box that keeps mice out of the house; but it often conks out in a rainstorm. For those deer that jump into the highway, there is a type of whistle that can be mounted on a car bumper. You can't hear the ultrasonic scream, but the deer can—sometimes, alas, too late.

Certainly a live-and-let-live attitude is preferable to encouraging even more hunting, with more hunters shooting one another and the rest of us. Deer are a lot less dangerous to the suburbanite than are fellow suburbanites with rifles and shotguns. Nor is any hunter I've seen as attractive as his quarry. Indeed, I find it difficult not to conclude that the whitetail deer, browsing the upper meadow or loping across the suburban landscape, is one of nature's noblest animals and well worth whatever nuisance it may cause.

SIX

Gulls on the Roof

THEY are outside my window now, nattering and bickering, crooning and pleading, whimpering and screeching. Some of them are feeding along the tide line, nipping at one another and contesting every clam and crab. Two of them wheel over the house, *kuck-kucking* as one tries to make the other drop its prize. A line of them perches on the peak of my neighbor's guano-spattered roof. Others are chorusing the *KEEEE-OOK-yukyukyukyuk* that is the universal sound of the seashore (and the dubbed-in sound effect of every movie scene set near the coast).

Watching seagulls in flight, their crisp white wings against the blue sky, others besides me have marveled at their graceful beauty. A Canadian literary magazine editor once complained that he received more poems about seagulls than about nearly any other subject (almost four hundred in one year). One of the most popular fictional characters of the last half-century was Richard Bach's high-flying, speed-diving Jonathan Livingston Seagull. And Ogden Nash chided the romantic aura of the gull with a memorable whimsy:

> Hark to the whimper of the sea-gull,
> He weeps because he's not an ea-gull.

Suppose you were, you silly sea-gull,
Could you explain it to your she-gull?

Actually the seagull is far from a romantic creature. It
is a tough, pragmatic bird that has adapted wonderfully to
the odious waste of our modern effluent society. The gulls'
prime feeding grounds are garbage dumps and shopping-
center parking lots. In England there are commuter gulls
that fly up to London to feed on scraps, returning at night
to the coast. In the United States the gulls that subsist on
garbage rear more chicks than those that remain on the
offshore islands.

Surrounded by them as I am, I couldn't resist reading
up on them, if only to enhance and explain some of my
puzzling observations. I quickly found that the family Laridae, to which the gulls belong, has been a popular subject
for ornithologists, who have spied on them, imprisoned,
painted, and poisoned them in thousands of experiments.
In the process they have found that the seagull is a most
remarkable critter.

One obvious finding is that "seagull" is a misnomer
for most of the forty-four species in the Laridae family.
Only a few gulls spend most of their time at sea. It is
mainly a shore bird. Even the great black-backed gull *Larus
marinus*, the largest of the Laridae, with nearly a six-foot
wingspan, hangs around the coast and the not-so-far-off-
shore islands.

There are gulls throughout most of the world. Some
venture as far north as the Arctic. Another species, the gray
gull, flies sixty miles inland from the Pacific coast to breed
in Chile's twelve-thousand-foot-high Atacama Desert,
where temperatures reach one hundred degrees Fahrenheit,
returning every night, riding the updrafts from the cooling
desert, to the Pacific for fish to bring back to their young.

(Their breeding ground was discovered in 1913 by a naturalist working for a nitrate company.) Their epic commutation—few gulls fly at night—has puzzled ornithologists; perhaps it is to get away from the kelp gull, a larger, predatory bird that inhabits the same area of the Pacific coast.

In the United States, the ring-billed gull generally prefers the Great Lakes, the western gull is found along the California coast, and the glaucous-winged gull is farther north, in the Pacific Northwest. The bird that epitomizes the word *seagull*, the herring gull *(Larus argentatus)*, has the greatest population of them all and flocks up and down the Atlantic coast.

Flock is a key word. Gulls of a feather do flock together, and establish a well-organized social system in which numbers provide protection, rank has its privileges, and male gulls constantly battle for dominance. One male, for example, will select the tallest piling and perch on it. He has hardly ruffled his feathers into place when a second male sweeps onto the scene. Although half a dozen other pilings are unoccupied, the newcomer will usually try to force the other off the tallest one. If he succeeds, he will strike an arrogant pose, head high, lord of all he surveys, while the loser settles on a lower piling, extending his neck and mewing in submission.

Battling gulls vividly demonstrate a rare avian versatility. Unlike most birds, they are almost equally adept at swimming, walking (even trotting), and flying. But it is in the air that they are in their element. Two gulls in an aerial fight over a juicy morsel of putrid fish can twist, turn, zoom, stall, and dive with a dexterity unmatched by most other birds. And the winner can snatch the falling piece of food in midair. Often when I am tossing bread to the local swans, half a dozen gulls will wheel onto the scene, picking off most of the crumbs in midair.

In a series of wind-tunnel experiments with laughing gulls *(Larus atricilla)*, an ornithologist measured their top speed at fifty miles per hour; at their cruising speed (nineteen miles per hour) they were more energy-efficient than a horse or an automobile. (The gulls appeared to enjoy the experiment.)

The same acrobatic gulls can also stretch their long wings and soar for hours. Man's most intricate engineering has produced nothing to match the aerodynamic qualities of the gull's wing. When a breeze pipes up over our cove, the dozen gulls floating outside my window look as if they were painted in the sky. Gulls will follow a ship far out to sea, riding the vessel's updraft, their feet tucked into their tail feathers to reduce drag, seemingly motionless until one suddenly whisks into action when a providential passenger tosses a scrap of food. A gull is so at home in the air that it can preen its chest or scratch its head while in flight.

Gulls can migrate over great distances; one herring gull banded at Isle of Shoals, New Hampshire, in July 1933, was shot in Panama five months later. But most of our local gulls seem content to remain in the neighborhood, though some apparently fly offshore to island breeding grounds less disturbed by human intruders. They prefer to winter, however, where the garbage is, and cold weather scarcely bothers them. The gull's feathers are layered to provide excellent insulation, and its feet are protected by miniature valves that pump warm blood to its webbed toes. When ice forms along the edge of our cove, the ducks usually swim out into the open water, their undersides insulated by layers of fat, while the gulls stand around on the ice. A sleeping gull often balances on one foot at a time, alternately warming the other against its body.

Although many of their migrating patterns have changed because of the garbage supply, gulls retain an uncanny sense of direction and a keen memory. When taken as far as three hundred miles from their habitat, most of them have flown straight home—some have even found shortcuts—because home is where the food is. And it can be almost any kind of food. Few critters could stomach the enormously varied diet of the gull. It can be carnivorous or vegetarian, depending on what's available. One gull, offered a varied menu in captivity while its broken wings healed, showed a preference for raw mice with a side order of mashed potatoes. Gulls in the wild have been seen devouring dead rats and blueberries, drowned kittens and oats, barnacles and barley, moths, midges, maggots, and pumpkin seeds. In 1848, flocks of gulls that strayed inland as far as Utah devoured nearly all the grasshoppers in the area; in gratitude for ending the plague, the Mormons erected a statue in Salt Lake City topped by two gulls (characteristically fighting).

Gulls can consume carrion so deadly that, in the opinion of one ornithologist, it would "kill a regiment." One fisherman surface-trolling on Long Island Sound found himself reeling in a gull and had to cut his line. The gull probably coughed up the lure later, hooks and all. The larger black-backed and herring gulls are merciless predators, even raiding nests of their own species. The day-old, still-wet chicks go down easily; the fluffy older ones are harder to swallow, but a determined gull can manage. Eider ducklings, which hatch on some of the same islands, are easy prey when they first enter the water. If the victim instinctively dives underwater for protection, the gulls wait patiently until it comes up for air.

Besides an iron stomach, the gull is equipped with a gaping bill and a huge gullet that can accommodate a third of the gull's weight. A Californian watched a gull climb into the sky with the wriggling feet of a rabbit protruding from its beak. I have not forgotten one dinner aboard a friend's boat, which was interrupted when a herring gull swept the large steak off his stern barbecue and just made it to the shore, where its friends awaited the feast. Large black-backed gulls have been known to carry off newborn ewes; smaller gulls are content to peck out the ewes' eyes. There is almost nothing a gull won't try to eat. A golfer in Atlanta, Georgia, saw an enterprising gull pluck his ball off the green, chomp on it, drop it to break it, and finally take it to the nearest water hazard to soak it before finally admitting defeat.

Gulls are among the few air-breathing creatures that can drink salt water; a special pair of glands in the gull's head extracts the salt and extrudes it in a saline solution from its beak. Gulls have excellent eyesight; riding the winds of a storm, they can watch from great heights for the dead fish and other edibles washed ashore by the waves. Seaside farmers are accustomed to being followed by gulls feasting on the worms and grubs turned up by the plow. Robins are frequently frustrated when gulls snatch away their fattest angleworms.

Gulls can detect and uncover crabs that have dug themselves into the sand. One of the comic spectacles of our cove is a line of gulls walking backwards, watching for the clams and other creatures that their feet have stirred up. Nearly as amusing, though not to the victim, is the scene at the beach when a picnicking toddler waves his peanut-butter sandwich in the air, only to have it picked off by a swooping gull. And every seaside road attests to the gull's ability to open a shellfish by dropping it on a hard surface.

Some ornithologists have characterized the gull as not overly bright. I'm not so sure. I have seen them repeatedly drop shells on a soft surface without catching on. Repetition seems not to teach some of them. A few years ago, the executives at Smith & Wesson's headquarters in Springfield, Massachusetts, had to close down a driving range because the gulls were swiping their golf balls and bombarding the players as they tried to break them. But Springfield is a long way up the Connecticut River from the sea, and the local gulls, less accustomed to saltwater clams, may not have realized that they didn't bounce like golf balls.

But some gulls are smarter than others—at least smarter than I am, which of course is no great claim. For years, while watching our gulls drop their clams and mussels, I wondered why they chose the busy road instead of the empty part of the parking lot, where they did not have to dodge the passing cars. Then one day I heard a crunching sound and realized the gulls' shrewdness. They were dropping their clams in front of the oncoming cars, then diving down to retrieve the shells smashed by the tires and gulp the contents.

Whether by intelligence or instinct, gulls gather for mutual protection during the spring breeding season. Selecting an isolated beach or island, they stake out their colony complete with boundaries, sentinels, and a gridwork of nesting sites. The daily din of territorial battles is ear-shattering; only at night does the uproar diminish to a low, murmuring chorus.

As new gulls arrive at the raucous colony, each male selects his patch of land and proclaims his ownership by strutting back and forth, his wings partly unfolded like hunched shoulders; sometimes the scene resembles a tryout for a few thousand Groucho Marx imitators. The male defends his territory fiercely. At the approach of a male intruder, he usually warns it off with what ornithologists call his "threat posture"—neck stretched, beak down, wings raised. If the trespasser doesn't get it, the defender gives him a more unmistakable warning, called "grass pull-

ing," pecking at the ground to demonstrate the damage he can do to the intruder's feathers. Sometimes large patches of beach grass are uprooted in such a display.

That is the final warning. If it doesn't have the desired effect, the battle is on. Both birds slash at each other with their wings and try to peck out each other's eyes and feathers. Naturalist Peter Pyle described one such encounter on a California island. "They grabbed each other's wings and bills and pulled. . . . They'd stop and pant awhile and then start again. I tried to stop it but couldn't. The fight went on for four or five hours. . . . The other birds stood about watching." The two gulls fought until they could stand no longer. The next day they were gone from the colony; Pyle believes both died of their wounds.

The winner, if he survives, periodically throws back his head and gives his "long call," as ornithologists describe it, to attract a mate. Shortly she arrives. Most gulls are monogamous, usually mating for life. The divorce rate has been estimated at about 3 to 5 percent a year. If the pair has been to this breeding ground the previous year, they usually have separated on leaving it. Now, with astonishing memory, both find their way back, recognize each other, and promptly start building their nest of twigs, leaves, and seaweed. Long puzzled by the gulls' ability to tell one from another, ornithologists finally discovered that the distinguishing feature is a colored circle around the gull's eye; by painting them differing shades, experimenters broke up many a happy gull marriage.

If the male is new to the breeding colony, or has just matured, he awaits a new mate. Unattached females come wheeling over the nesting sites, like debutantes assessing the stag line. When one spies an attractive prospect, she alights, flutters her tail feathers, and minces up and down in front of him. Seagulls are not subtle. If the male does not fancy this female, he drives her away. But if he is intrigued, he lets her stay.

As she struts before him, she looks away, then peeks back over her shoulder at him. If he moves toward her, she coquettishly dances a few feet away. She may even fly off. The male responds with another long call, which brings her back—unless she has meanwhile spotted a more appealing bachelor. This taunting procedure can occur again and again for a few days before she finally decides that this gull is for her.

Now she takes the initiative, crooning and nuzzling him and gently stroking the underside of his bill. At first he ignores, or pretends to ignore, her advances. But she continues to importune him, mewing and stroking his neck. If he retreats, she follows him, rubbing against him, caressing his bill, and muttering low, throaty gurgles of invitation until finally the male can stand it no longer. He throws up.

That is his signal of surrender; by feeding her this regurgitated food, he shows that he accepts her. Besides a symbolic signal of pair bonding, it is an assurance that he will provide her with the sustenance she will need to nurture her eggs. They start to build a nest; they may not actually copulate for a couple of weeks. Three weeks after that, she deposits her fertile eggs, usually two or three, in the nest.

While studying these mating rites on California's Santa Barbara Island some years ago, zoologists George and Molly Hunt made a curious discovery. Some of the nests had too many eggs. The normal number is three, but these nests contained twice as many. Moreover, few of these eggs produced chicks.

Why? In response to some environmental threat? If so, why weren't they hatching? It took four years for the Hunts to solve the mystery. First they trapped the gulls at what they called the "supernormal clutches." Nearly all of them turned out to be female. As a control, they trapped some of the gulls on the nests with the normal numbers of eggs; they were the usual pairings of male and female.

Since even an ornithologist has trouble identifying the sex of a gull at a distance, the Hunts next identified the sexes of their subjects with different colors and settled down to watch their mating behavior. Thus came the solution.

Santa Barbara Island, they discovered, unlike any other nesting area studied, had a small but distinct population (about 14 percent of the colony) of lesbian gulls. Not only were pairs of females staking out territories and building nests; both were also laying their infertile eggs and vainly trying to incubate them. (That explained the nests with double the normal numbers of eggs.) Most of these female pairs went through the usual motions of courtship, with one female assuming the male role; some even attempted copulation. And while one female sat on the nest doing her best to cover half a dozen eggs, her partner defended the territory and went in search for food.

"We were absolutely astounded," George Hunt said. "This sort of thing has not been found before. . . . Homosexual pairing has not, to our knowledge, been reported for any group of wild birds."

Their studies were complicated when they found that a few of the lesbian pairs' eggs were fertile. That problem was solved when they observed an occasional infidelity on the part of neighboring males. But, aside from a possible reaction to a preponderance of female gulls, the Hunts could find no satisfactory reason for the behavior of these gay gulls. Perhaps a simple explanation is that the birds are Californians.

Fertilized gull eggs are mottled and almost perfectly camouflaged; but even then they have only about a fifty-fifty chance of hatching. They are regarded as choice morsels by innumerable predators, including other gulls. If one clutch of eggs is destroyed, however, the female can lay another. And after a month of incubation, the first chick pecks its way out with a special "egg tooth." As soon as it has freed itself, the parents toss the empty shell fragments out of the nest so that the white insides of the shells will not attract more predators. Within days the other chicks emerge; often the third is the runt of the hatching. Its siblings, with only a few days' head start, grow so rapidly that they dominate the nest.

During their first weeks the chicks continue to be imperiled by trespassers—foxes, raccoons, hedgehogs, wea-

sels, snakes, crows, ravens, and skuas and other sea birds.
Sometimes, ironically, the chicks are blown out of their
nests by the environmentalists' helicopters. Although life
in the colony may seem chaotic, there is some order in the
pandemonium. A bird or animal sneaking up on the area
promptly discovers the gulls' efficient alarm system. The
first gull to spot danger lets out a special warning yelp that
sets the entire colony screaming. Often the gulls gang up
to drive the intruder away. One naturalist trying to study
a gulls' breeding area had to retreat (minus his hat) after
being dive-bombed and plastered with guano. The older,
dominant gulls stake out their territories in the center of
the colony where it is safest.

But danger can also come from within, with gulls in
the colony attacking one another. Ornithologist Nikolaas
Tinbergen, after studying gull colonies for thirty years,
concluded that some gulls attack other gulls for no apparent
reason other than just for the hell of it. Gulls gobble up
their neighbors' chicks, especially during the first few days,
when the chicks are too young to hide; unable to identify
their parents and hoping for food, they rush to greet their
killers.

So about half of the eggs do not hatch, and about half
of the chicks do not live long. But the survivors mature
rapidly. On each parent's bill is a red spot at which the
chick pecks, stimulating the parent to disgorge the food it
has brought back to the nest. (When experimenters painted
out the spot, the chicks stopped feeding.) After about a
month, a young gull is ready to fly away from the breeding
colony and is nearly full grown. I have seen plenty of
ducklings and cygnets on our cove, but never a gull chick.

The young gull is distinguished, however, by its plumage, which takes three years to fade from mottled brown
to the pure white of the adult. The full-sized gull finally

has virtually no predators. No diseases are endemic to the family Laridae (though you'd think they'd have permanent gastroenteritis); its species is resistant even to the effects of DDT. When some ornithologists tried feeding gull chicks normally lethal doses of crude oil to test their survivability in tanker spills, the oil merely slowed their growth. One airline pilot discovered how tough a gull can be when he landed at Washington's National Airport and watched one stagger out of the plane's engine cowling, shake its head, and fly away.

Boat owners in our cove have long since learned the gull's adaptability. Some sailors install whirling rods on their decks to scare the gulls away and keep them from fouling the decks; the gulls simply lean against one arm of the rod, immobilizing it. Gulls also appear to learn fast. An Oregonian who regularly fed them at his office window discovered during a Saturday visit that they knew it was a weekend and didn't bother to show up. It is no wonder that gulls live to a ripe old age. Many that have been banded have lived long after the metal strips on their legs have rusted away. Twenty-year-old gulls are common in the wild. And the gull thrives in captivity; the oldest known died in a Moorehead City, North Carolina, aviary just before reaching its fiftieth birthday.

It is difficult to believe that the hardy Laridae nearly became extinct about a century ago. They had survived gullnappers in England and Labrador, who fattened them like geese for the table, as well as egg-hunters in New England. Even the early naturalists shot their specimens to study them. John James Audubon killed and stuffed many of the gulls he portrayed in his famous paintings. (He also tried eating them, but found them too salty.) But the gull that was more than a match for the hunters and egg collectors was nearly done in by the nineteenth-century lady of fashion.

After the popular *Godey's Lady's Book* featured the newest craze for feathered hats in 1875, the *grandes dames* of the Gilded Age went so far as to decorate their hats with entire birds. One naturalist in 1896 made his own census among New York's smart set: 542 hats representing forty different species of birds. And as white became the favorite color, the gun-toting agents of New York's milliners devastated the gull population of the East Coast. By 1899 the price had soared to three dollars per gull, and the American seagull was on the verge of extinction.

In 1866 the editor of *Forest and Stream* magazine, with the likely name of George Bird Grinnell, had proposed "an Association for the protection of wild birds and their eggs, which shall be called the Audubon Society." But the shooting went on until a determined band of Boston women, heaping scorn on their feather-hatted friends, lobbied their representatives to push through Congress in 1916 a Migratory Bird Treaty protecting the birds from their human predators.

The resilient gull recovered rapidly. There were an estimated ten thousand herring gulls along the East Coast in 1899; today they are beyond count. The gull is a testimonial to nature's adaptability—and, to some, a mixed blessing. Gulls clean our beaches, and their droppings fertilize coastal pastures. But predatory gulls threaten other species, especially the smaller terns (also of the family Laridae). Naturalists have tried to keep the gulls from invading the tern breeding grounds, with indifferent success. Attempts to puncture their eggs have failed when the gulls laid a second clutch. One project became counterproductive when an amateur destroyed an entire tern colony by mistake. Gulls have quickly learned to refuse poisoned bait.

And they have threatened their major benefactor, the origin of the refuse on which they subsist. Hundreds of human fatalities have been caused by gulls swarming on airport runways and getting sucked into jet engines. "Gull patrols" at airports have worked only temporarily. No island could be better designed as a gull rookery than Logan International Airport in Boston, Massachusetts, which is surrounded by fishing vessels and contains a huge garbage dump. Noisemakers and shotguns have driven the gulls away only until the noisemaking stopped.

At New York's Kennedy International Airport, according to one study, nearly 3,400 planes collided with birds between 1979 and 1992; some fifty of the planes were damaged. Airport officials tried everything from plastering gulls' eggs with oil to driving the birds away with cannon fire. When the guns went off, the gulls flew away; when the firing ceased, they were found perching on the cannon. In desperation—and despite loud protests from bird-lovers—the officials shotgunned some thirty thousand gulls in 1991 and 1992. But even that slaughter destroyed only a quarter of the local gull population; more kept coming, most of them from a wildlife refuge unfortunately situated next to the airport.

Considering such a nuisance factor, as well as the gulls' raucous, aggressive behavior, it is no surprise that they occasionally have a bad press. Naturalist Janet Hopson referred to them as "unmitigated thugs of the bird world." William Leon Dawson branded the western gull as "cruel of beak and bottomless of maw." Even the Boswell of the gull, ornithologist Tinbergen, in his classic *The Herring Gull's World*, described a gull rookery as "a city of thieves and murderers."

Still, the gull has its defenders. Zoologist William Drury points out that gulls are "no more predatorial than many others. They're just easier to see because of where they are." Indeed, they are nearly omnipresent. Disapprobation has done little to curb their population. The gull is one critter that belongs near the top of the *un*endangered list; the most numerous species, the herring gull, has doubled its population every dozen years since 1900. But it has finally slowed its growth, not because of man's efforts at control, but because man's massive waste is not enough for the voracious gull.

I'm glad to hear that. Watching what seemed an ever-growing swarm of gulls in our cove, I had begun to wonder when they might take over. Now, if the ornithologists are correct, I can relax and enjoy these independent, utilitarian, clever, beautiful birds. Certainly the gulls, for all their bickering and battling, seem to enjoy themselves, especially when the wind is blowing. Looking skyward at a flock of them soaring in glorious circles, I realize that I, too, would far rather be a seagull than an ea-gull.

SEVEN

A Mockingbird on the Antenna

Wʜᴀᴛ I like most about our resident mockingbird is that he probably came north on Interstate 95.

Not many years ago the mockingbird was a rarity in our part of the country. Bird books reported that they had spread across most of the United States, but a mockingbird sighting in Connecticut was enough to bring out the bird-watchers to add it to their life lists. At the turn of the century the amateur naturalist Teddy Roosevelt recalled that when he was a boy, a mockingbird on Long Island was a *rara avis*. In 1939, ornithologist Edward Howe For-bush gave the mockingbird's range as "sparingly north to New York and Massachusetts." And as recently as 1960, an Audubon Society bird count in our town turned up not a single mockingbird. That same year ornithologist Henry Hill Collins, Jr., was asking, "Can anyone visualize the gray-clad aristocrat amid snow and ice, amid spruces and hemlocks, or upon cliffs battered by the might of the North Atlantic?" The mockingbird was, and by some ornitholo-gists still is, regarded as a southern bird. Indeed, it is the official bird of five states—Arkansas, Florida, Mississippi, Tennessee, and Texas—all of them southern.

But even as naturalist Collins was posing his rhetorical

question, the mockingbird was making its move north. And when highway engineers planted multiflora rosebushes on the median dividers of such interstate thruways as I-95, running from Florida to Maine, the mockingbirds, feeding on the rose hips, followed the bushes north as they were planted. Ornithologist Richard M. De Grasf claims that they swarmed up through New England in only eight years. And still they come, including, I assume, the serenading critter in our yard. Of course, he may be a first- or second-generation New Englander; a couple of friends claim that he has no southern accent, but I think they are kidding me. In any case, his immediate ancestors must have made the pilgrimage north along the thruway.

And not just to New England. Nowadays there are various subspecies all across the United States, the western versions being slightly larger and paler but just as vocal. There are other species from Saskatchewan all the way to Tierra del Fuego, including one indigenous only to the Galapagos Islands; in fact, one expert, Frank J. Sullaway, has argued that it was the Galapagos mockingbirds, not the finches, that helped start Charles Darwin on the track of his theory of evolution.

What I also like about our mockingbird is his personality. From reading up on the species, I assume he is a male, because it's hard to tell the sexes apart by appearance. The female, I read, can be combative. But probably no bird is as pugnacious as the male mockingbird. And certainly our mockingbird is the feistiest character in the neighborhood. This is no small claim; a few years ago we had a catbird that enjoyed chasing cats.

The mockingbird, a cousin of the catbird, is even more aggressive. Ours has attacked crows three times his size. When he swoops down onto our birdbath, grackles scatter. He usurps the bird feeder and sometimes even drives the squirrels from theirs. Some ornithologists credit the rapid incursion of the mockingbirds to their appropriation of bird feeders throughout the North. Naturalist Charlton Ogburn reported that he was forced to trap and remove his local mockingbird to keep the other birds from starving.

The biggest bully of all is the mockingbird defending his turf—or trying to seize territory from another mockingbird. A favorite battleground of our mockingbird is the seawall, where his confrontations are awesome. I've marveled annually at the ferocity with which attacker and defender go at each other. The battle usually starts with a prancing minuet while the two birds, tails high, spar with each other. Then comes wing-flashing, a unique mockingbird gesture that exposes the white underparts of the wings in a jerky motion, as if the bird were battery-operated. Then one will lunge at the other, rather like a prizefighter jabbing at his opponent. And then the flying fury as the two come together in a swirling cloud of feathers. Separating, glaring, and wing-flashing, they pause only for a few seconds before hurtling at each other again.

Mockingbirds have been known to rupture an aorta or have a heart attack during such battles. Ornithologists report witnessing the spectacular melee of half a dozen mockingbirds swirling about in one flying dogfight. But on our seawall the conflict usually ends after a few furious minutes, with the loser flying away and the victor prancing back and forth, jerking his wings in triumph.

Mockingbirds defending their territory attack not only invading birds but anything they consider a threat. They have flattened themselves against windows, mirrors, or hubcaps, unaware that they are attacking their own reflections. They are undaunted even by humans; some years ago the postmen in Houston, Texas, refused to make their deliveries in one neighborhood where dive-bombing mock-ingbirds were terrorizing everyone in sight.

Naturalist Janet Lembke muses that it may be more than territorial. "I also suspect," she writes, "that mockers grab space just for the hell of it," and describes her mock-ingbird's delight in hopping along the porch railing to nip at the tail of her sleeping cat. A dive-bombing mockingbird, uttering its strident *tchak*, *tchak* as if mimicking a machine gun, is a frightening sight. Dogs whose owners unwittingly stationed their doghouses near a mockingbird's nest have been attacked and effectively imprisoned in their kennels. Kit and George Harrison report on a family of mocking-birds that attacked a local cat every time it went outdoors, until the victim became so paranoid that it refused to leave the house. Another naturalist, William H. McHenry, re-counted a story of one cat's Pyrrhic revenge. After numer-ous attacks on the feline's tail, a mockingbird made the mistake of diving at its head. The cat leaped into the air, mouth agape, and left nothing but a few feathers drifting to the ground. Unwisely, or perhaps in its rage, the cat chomped down the entire bird and shortly died of a stom-ach obstruction.

But what makes our mockingbird most attractive, of course, is his lilting, soaring symphony of song. His scien-tific name comes from his singing. The mockingbird be-longs to the Mimidae, a bird family of mimics (*mimus* is Latin for "mimic") including thrushes, brown thrashers, and catbirds. The mockingbird not only outmocks but out-sings them all, and is accordingly named *Mimus polyglottos* (Greek for "many-tongued"). Yale ornithologists Charles Sibley and Jon Ahlquist think that the Mimidae may have evolved more than 20 million years ago from an ancestor rather like the starling.

The Mimidae family is native only to the Americas;

when the first visiting European naturalists heard the mockingbird, they could scarcely believe their ears. The Scottish artist Alexander Wilson marveled at the mockingbird's imitations of every bird from the "mellow notes of the wood thrush to the savage scream of the eagle." The American mockingbird, he wrote, is "unrivaled by the feathered species of this or perhaps any other country." Englishmen have called the mockingbird "America's nightingale"; one German ornithologist considered the former superior to the latter, arguing that the nightingale did not have the "finishing talent" of the mockingbird. Naturalist John Burroughs agreed, calling the mockingbird "the lark and the nightingale in one." Artist John James Audubon crowned it the "king of song." One of my favorite accolades was that of the Texas legislature when it selected its state bird. The mockingbird, the declaration stated, is "a singer of distinctive type, a fighter for the protection of his home, falling, if need be, in its defense, like any true Texan."

The mockingbird does not have the color of the cardinal or the woodpecker. It is a drab, robin-sized bird with a distinctive, perky long tail and gray wings that flash white in flight. But it makes up for its drabness with its song. As its name suggests, the mockingbird mocks every bird within earshot—and some it remembers; one ornithologist noted this as long ago as 1912, when he heard a mockingbird imitate the song of the tanager, which had not yet migrated to the area for the season. Experts have counted nearly a hundred different bird calls repeated by this mimic, with another hundred or two of its own. American Indians called it the *cencontlatolly,* meaning "four hundred tongues." The Navajo, Hopi, Paiute, Shoshone, and some other tribes believed that the mockingbird gave their ancestors their voices as they emerged from the underworld into North America.

Samuel Grimes, who has recorded mockingbirds for nearly two decades, clocked one warbling 310 different tunes in fifteen minutes, including 114 calls from twenty-nine other birds. So realistic are their imitations that mockingbirds have been shot by hunters who thought they had heard a dove or a quail. Indeed, some of the birds themselves cannot tell they are being mimicked, and answer the mockingbird's call.

But the mockingbird does more than just plagiarize. While most birds have simple one-to-three-note calls, the mockingbird orchestrates them into a veritable symphony that can go on for hours with only brief pauses for rest. Its cousin the brown thrasher has a much larger repertoire, but it consists mainly of imitations, while the mockingbird melds them into far more melodious song.

All other birdsong in the area seems to fade as the mockingbird sounds forth. It dominates the scene by seizing the highest possible perch for its broadcast. Our mockingbird's favorite site is atop the TV antenna. I have watched and listened to him vocalize for as much as five minutes, evidently without catching a breath, synchronizing his own notes with those of the local robins, crows, thrushes, and gulls, sometimes interspersed with the honk of a Canada goose. Something like:

Terrildee, terrildee, terrildee,
Chirp, chirp, chirp, chirp,
Releeto, releeto, releeto,
Honk, honk, honk, honk,
Kiree, kiree, kiree, kiree,
Rumbletree, rumbletree, rumbletree,
Eeyou, eeyou, eeyou,
Speero, speero, speero,
Caw, caw, caw, caw . . .

Much of the charm of Alice Hawthorne's song "Listen to the Mockingbird," with its haunting picture of the bird singing over a loved one's grave, is in the evocative rhythm of the chorus, so much like that of the mockingbird itself.

Often our mockingbird's performance is as impressive to see as to hear. Perched atop the antenna, he swells his chest and lets go, swaying with the melody of his song. As it reaches a crescendo he literally rises with it, flapping his wings and soaring above his perch. With a triumphant swoop, he lands on the seawall or the lawn, where he struts back and forth, sometimes flashing the whites of his wings, as if awaiting applause.

The applause he is looking for is from a mate-to-be. Ornithologists argue about why a mockingbird makes such a magnificent fuss. Most agree that while birdsong has its utilitarian functions—establishing territory, attracting mates, warning of danger—some of the time birds sing merely for the pleasure of it. Clearly, ours enjoys it. Some experts also maintain that the male, in staking out his territory, is warning the other birds away by fooling them into believing that the place is swarming with all sorts of species. At the same time, other experts believe, the mockingbird is sending a mating signal: a female cruising about looking for a mate is inclined to believe that the male with the largest repertoire has seized the largest territory.

I have often wondered what she makes of his other mimicry. Our mockingbird gives excellent imitations of barking squirrels, auto horns, police and fire sirens, the local foghorn, the neighborhood's many different burglar alarms, and even my chain saw. The one local noise he has not yet copied is the howl of the leaf-blower. Perhaps he knows that if he tried it, he might explode in the attempt.

Often the mockingbird's excellent mimicry causes confusion. An ornithologist in Louisiana recalled an imita-

tion of a dinner bell so realistic that the field workers came in early for lunch. Other mockingbirds mimic crickets, frogs, dogs, and cats. The audience at an outdoor concert of the National Symphony Orchestra in Washington, D.C., thought they were hearing an echo when a nearby mockingbird joined in, mimicking the flute mimicking the bird in *Peter and the Wolf*. (With human complacency I used to consider the symphony the finest example of man's intellectual superiority over the beast—until I realized that the mockingbird was more versatile than any human musician.)

The mockingbird seems particularly eloquent in Texas, perhaps because there are so many of them there. Naturalist

Roy Bedichek claims that the area "supports more mockingbirds per acre than any other." I recall that during a late May visit to a friend's ranch in Texas's hill country, the local mockingbirds outchirped, outsang, and outscreeched the entire avian population with the exception of a pair of screaming peacocks. (The mockingbirds also tried to imitate them, but without achieving the same volume). As ours does in Greenwich, especially during a warm spring evening, the Texas mockingbirds sang on into the darkness, when all the other birds had bedded down in their nests. In fact, the Texas mockingbirds even woke some of the other birds, who joined in to fill the night with unwonted—and, after a few nights, unwanted—song.

In the eighteenth and nineteenth centuries the mockingbird's song was nearly its undoing. Because they thrived and continued to sing in captivity, there was a widespread fad for caged mockingbirds. When Thomas Jefferson, the widowed president, was alone evenings in the White House, he released his pet mockingbird to sit on his desk and sing for him while he went over his papers; at bedtime it hopped up the stairs after him to the presidential bedroom. Mockingbirds in gilded cages sailed to Europe and Asia to entertain the wealthy, and incidentally to propagate the species abroad. (There is a theory that some of the ancestors of Britain's mockingbirds actually flew across the Atlantic.) They were not perfect pets; one British bird fancier complained about the "pleasure which they took in scaring their associates" in his aviary.

There was also a lively market in the United States during the nineteenth century, with fledglings selling for five dollars and adult birds in full voice bringing twenty-five dollars, a huge sum in those times. But many died of neglect; a caged mockingbird requires about a dozen spiders a day and has a tendency toward diarrhea. After a considerable cry from bird-lovers, the Audubon Society lobbied successfully for laws protecting mockingbirds along with many others that were endangered at the turn of the century.

But *Mimus polyglottos* still appears to enjoy and in fact to prefer the company of *Homo sapiens*. Certainly the mockingbird has no fear of humans; it will as readily attack a man or woman as it would any smaller intruder. Mockingbirds especially like TV antennas, peaked roofs, utility poles, fenceposts, walks, porches, and the other amenities of human civilization—not to mention the occasional dog or cat to chase. And suburbanites also provide the mockingbird with its favorite multiflora roses as well as other garden shrubs that shelter the birds' nests.

By early spring the male mockingbird has shopped about and chosen and staked out his territory, which he proceeds to proclaim with song. He usually starts modestly with a few selections sung from the bush he has chosen for a nest site. Whether attracted by his singing or also looking around, other males fly into his territory, to be met with a fierce defense. Meanwhile, as the territorial male's testes swell, his song swells too, and he flies to the highest peak of his territory to announce his availability for a mate. His repertoire now expands exponentially, until no female within hundreds of yards can remain unimpressed.

After doing her own shopping around to inspect the various males in the neighborhood, a female makes a tentative appearance in this territory. She is greeted by a symphony of song—and by what looks like a threat. Because it is so difficult to tell the sexes apart, I often confused this preliminary courtship with the male's defense against other males. Perhaps, I thought, he has a hard time telling the difference too. But after a few more seasons of mockingbird-watching, I realized that initially the two sexes squared off in almost the same way. They then go into a courtship dance, tails erect, facing and circling each other, hopping side by side, apparently while trying to make up their minds. It is rare for the male to be choosy. The female is more likely to fly off and continue her inspection of other sites and suitors. If she returns, it may be too late; the next female visitor may have decided to move in.

Whichever female accepts the male's serenading proposal, the male's loud calls become more subdued, in what one ornithologist termed a "happy, contented-sounding" song. Then the pair usually joins in a love duet, harmonizing in a soft, modulated *hew, hew, hew* to signify their new bond. One ornithologist studied six pairs of bonded mockingbirds and concluded that this lower-decibel song, on the male's part, is pure seduction, designed to lure the female into the mating mood. In any case, the duet is often resumed while the pair mate and set about building their nest.

In this domestic duty the female promptly asserts her authority, inspecting the site the male has chosen and perhaps rejecting it for one she prefers. It is usually low for a bird's nest, not more than ten feet above the ground. The favorite venue is a dense shrub or vine, or the lower branches of a tree. The household duties are now properly divided, with the male fetching the nest materials, which the female approves of or rejects. Both may work at the actual construction, with the female deciding where everything goes. The nest usually consists of a platform and an outer layer of sturdy twigs, lined with moss, grass, leaves, hair, string, or cotton that the male has found. The work goes speedily; the nest is completed in four or five days, whereupon the female promptly settles into it and lays her first egg, a small oval of blue-green mottled with brown. In succeeding days she lays three or four more, which she incubates by herself, leaving the nest only briefly to eat during the two weeks of incubation. The male stands guard, continuing to serenade her and announce to all possible intruders his "no trespassing" signal.

Baby mockingbirds emerging from their shell are blind and featherless, barely able to hold up their tiny beaks for the food that both parents bring them. The first meals consist of easily swallowed bits of worm or a soft, wriggling caterpillar. But within a couple of weeks the young birds are able to swallow and digest grubs, crickets, and even thrashing grasshoppers. In less than a fortnight they are hopping about in the nest; some of them topple out, to the screaming consternation of their parents, who try, usually in vain, to drive off the cats that pounce on them—no doubt savoring, as much as the tasty meal, the sweet revenge after weeks of harassment from the parents.

Among the other predators of mockingbird eggs and hatchlings are hawks, gulls, crows, raccoons, skunks, opossums, and snakes. One of Audubon's most dramatic paintings depicts a mockingbird family attacking a snake that has invaded their nest. Some 70 percent of mockingbirds do not survive to adulthood. Those that do survive live an average of five years before being killed; mockingbirds rarely die of old age. The suburbs may be unthreatening for some critters but can be dangerous places for birds. Pampered in captivity, one mockingbird lived fifteen years.

The fledgling mockingbirds still have not changed their brown plumage to gray when they first learn to fly. But already their parents are leaving them to fend for themselves, because it is time to raise a new brood. Most mockingbirds raise two broods per season; some raise three. The entire procedure, from bonding through brooding, takes less than a month, so there is plenty of time for two. Shortly they have selected a site for a new nest. Mockingbirds are fussy about their nests, never reusing the old one. Some have been known to build and abandon as many as five in a season. And while they are incubating their second clutch, the fledglings of the first are off selecting their own territories and mates and adding to the cacophony of song all through the neighborhood.

Though most mockingbirds are monogamous, there is occasional polygamy. Ornithologists in North Carolina studied a couple of territories in which one of the males died. His neighbor took on his domestic duties, raising two broods with the widow and returning frequently to his own mate and young. Another male, in Florida, was seen to invite a second female into his territory, sufficiently removed from his first mate. This male, whom the ornithologists took to calling "the supermocker," successfully carried on his bigamous life through the breeding and incubating season. It wasn't easy. He was apparently occupied full-time in helping to feed the young of his second mate until they were fledged. He then flew back to help with the first brood, one of which by that time had starved. With both parents feeding them, the rest survived.

The watchers also marveled at the supermocker's violent defense of both nesting sites; on occasion he even drove intruders away from the territories of neighboring males. He may not have been so much a super mockingbird as a confused one. The observers also noted that he had gone through two previous breeding seasons singing without attracting a mate. (If you hear a mockingbird still singing late in the season, he is probably a lonely bachelor.)

North Carolina birdwatchers reported on a female mockingbird that carried on liaisons with two males in adjacent territories. She got away with it over a number of years, building four nests and raising six young. Evidently there was a preponderance of males in the area, so the two males accepted a sharing arrangement—when normally each would have been strongly protective of his female—rather than take the chance of having no mate at all.

In August, when the mating and waiting and fledging are over, the mockingbirds finally fall silent. The female often gives a last trilling call, as if to celebrate her new freedom, and both she and her mate subside. But not for long. By late September or early October the male starts singing again, this time to announce a new winter territory. He and his mate have taken up separate housekeeping, each usually in a smaller area rich in fruit-bearing trees and bushes. Their spring and summer diet of insects has changed to holly, blackberrry, mulberry, and bayberry. Some of my neighbors who feed them during the winter have found that they like sliced apples and figs, raisins, bread crumbs, and doughnuts. They also like grapes; those of a vintner in Florida attracted so many mockingbirds that he killed one thousand of them in trying to protect his crop.

When our mockingbird and his mate disappeared, I at first guessed that they had migrated south for the winter. But unlike their cousins the catbird and the brown thrasher, the mockingbird, once it has come north, tends to stay. And no doubt the mockingbirds I found in a nearby holly grove in January were the ones I had watched atop my TV antenna in June.

Often a pair of mockingbirds will establish their winter quarters next to each other, occasionally visiting across the borders, but defending them fiercely from any renegades that have not found their own winter territories and are trying to raid their neighbors. Sometimes the male mockingbird will stake out a smaller winter area inside his spring and summer territory, again inviting or tolerating visits only by his mate from her neighboring plot. Then, as winter phases into spring and the days get longer, the pair will move back into the territory they used the previous year. If by chance either has died, the other will seek out a new mate.

I have neighbors who complain—as sometimes I have—about raccoons in the garbage, deer in the orchard, and Canada geese on the fairway. But few of my friends complain about the mockingbirds, even when one erupts late on a still summer night. Mockingbirds do like grapes, and don't distinguish between wild and home-grown berries. But rarely do they feed in flocks like those in the Florida vineyard. And when we consider that during the growing season these birds consume such destructive insects as chinch bugs, boll weevils, cotton worms, cucumber beetles, and grasshoppers—not to mention flies, mosquitoes, and wasps—the balance is in their favor.

Looking out from his balcony in the White House, Harry Truman mused in his diary, "A robin hops around looking for worms, finds one and pulls with all his might to unearth him. A mockingbird imitates robins, jays, redbirds, crows, hawks—but has no individual note of his own. A lot of people like that."

For once Harry Truman was wrong; the mockingbird originates much more than it copies. I prefer the sentiment of Harper Lee. In *To Kill a Mockingbird*, the narrator's father, presenting his children with air rifles, says, "I'd rather you shot at tin cans in the backyard, but I know you'll go after birds. Shoot all the bluejays you want, if you can hit 'em, but remember it's a sin to kill a mockingbird."

Puzzled at the distinction, the narrator quizzes a neighbor, who explains it. "Your father's right. Mockingbirds don't do one thing but make music for us to enjoy.

They don't eat up people's gardens, don't nest in corn cribs, they don't do one thing but sing their hearts out for us. That's why it's a sin to kill a mockingbird."

I'm not sure what Harper Lee had against blue jays (though they do screech a lot). And I recognize that the mockingbird atop my TV antenna is singing his heart out not for me but for a female mockingbird. Nonetheless, still awed by his performance after all these years, I must agree that—thousands of cats to the contrary notwithstanding—Harper Lee was right.

EIGHT

Rabbits in the Garden

FOR an instant it was there; in the blink of an eye it was gone. I was on an early-morning bicycle ride through Greenwich Point, our town's combined beach and park, and the home of hundreds of rabbits. This one was in plain view near the road. Clearly it had seen me first. The moment I stopped for a closer look, it vanished as if clicked out like a light.

I had been observing the Point's rabbits for many years, and had started reading up on them. So, when this rabbit seemed to vanish into thin air, I thought I had the explanation. Rabbits, I had read, are accomplished burrowers, digging intricate series of tunnels for their warrens. Besides a main entrance, they provide a number of bolt holes, often hidden by tall grasses, down which they can instantly escape from danger. For a few months I enjoyed the notion of a community of rabbits swarming beneath the ground I walked and rode on. But after some more reading I was disillusioned.

The British rabbit (not to be confused with the hare, about which more later) does indeed burrow underground. But what I have been watching is the New England cottontail, which is content simply to hollow out a "form," as it is called, a rabbit-sized depression in which it hunkers down, ears laid back and body motionless, so it is hidden in the grass. My rabbit, then, had scampered with lightning speed into its form and disappeared.

I had probably interrupted its feeding for the rest of the day. But it was about finished anyway. Most rabbits in the wild are seminocturnal, so this one had been eating off and on since dusk of the previous day, and was topping off its dinner with a tossed salad of dew-drenched grass clippings from one of the town's lawnmowers. The rabbit would spend the rest of the daylight hours napping in its form, no doubt surrounded by other rabbits in their own beds, also undetectable to my unpracticed eye. On a bright day it might venture out of hiding, its keen eyes, nose, and long ears on the lookout for danger while it basked in the sun. But most of its day would be spent in hiding.

Had I wanted to, I could have walked through this rabbit village and sent a dozen of them scattering. Occasionally a dog will romp into such a community, nose down, following a rabbit trail, and stir up the inhabitants. I've never seen such an incursion. (Greenwich dogs are banned from Greenwich Point in the summer; the rabbits seem to know that). But when it does occur, I've read, a lookout rabbit generally signals the others with a great thump of its powerful hind legs. The entire population runs away, each in a different direction, at great speed and with zigzagging evasive action, leaving the dog, usually not one of the more intelligent animals, utterly bewildered. One by one, the rabbits slip through the nearest dense brush to safety.

The Greenwich Point rabbits, I have observed, have also learned to be selective about danger. In their evening and early-morning feeding forays, while humans are still about, they munch away contentedly alongside the road while autos pass, but they quickly disperse if one stops or a walker approaches. One of my neighbors reports that a rabbit took up residence in a bush near his front door. It kept an eye out for the lawnmower, frisky children, and other potential perils, but otherwise settled in.

A canny critter. The rabbit and its cousin the hare belong to the order Lagomorpha (meaning "hare-shaped") and the family Leporidae. They once were classed with rodents but have been found to be quite different, their major distinguishing feature being two sets of special teeth, a large forward row to crop food and smaller chewing molars behind them. Our New England leporids come in two species, the northern snowshoe hare and my neighbors, the New England cottontail, a subspecies of the eastern cottontail seen throughout most of the United States and parts of Canada and Central America.

Zoologists generally agree that the rabbit came to the Americas from Europe. Evidently they originated in Spain; there were rabbits and hares on Roman-Spanish coins at the time of the emperor Hadrian. (There are also reports of rabbits being used in religious ceremonies in China in the fifth century B.C.) They were apparently domesticated in Europe as early as the first century B.C. Julius Caesar mentions hares in his *Gallic Wars*, and the Roman writer Varro reported that they were raised in *leporaria*, walled garden enclosures, for their fur and meat. The Romans took them on their expeditions into northern Europe and spread them abroad. They were also taken aboard sailing ships as a fresh food supply for the crews, and those that reached land rapidly populated the vessels' destinations.

Our rabbits' ancestors may have evolved more than 50 million years ago. Archaeologists have turned up bones and teeth of rabbitlike animals in Asia as well as in North America, which suggests that, like the American Indians, there were American rabbits to meet the invading European rabbits when they crossed the Atlantic.

But they weren't called rabbits at first; the name evidently stems from the French *rabet*. Earlier, in Old French, the name was *connin*, and for centuries they were called *coneys*; only young coneys were called rabbits. New York's Coney Island was so named because at the time it was home to a lot of rabbits.

Considering rabbits' well-deserved reputation for proliferation, it is not surprising that they are nearly everywhere. In the Arctic there is a polar rabbit, white year-round (except for black ear tips) and so well insulated that it is uncomfortable in mild weather. The North American snowshoe hare is so called because in winter it grows bushy hair on its feet that helps it hop through soft snow and provides traction on ice. There is a silver-gray woolly hare that can survive above sixteen thousand feet in the Himalayas. There is a tiny volcano hare, only about a foot long, with no tail, that inhabits some Mexican volcanoes. In the Southwest desert of the United States there is a blacktail jackrabbit (Americans call hares jackrabbits), which has enormous ears that, radiatorlike, disperse the animal's heat. And there is an American white-sided jackrabbit that can ruffle its white side fur over its back as a warning of danger.

Rabbits and hares are such close cousins that a lot of my friends make no distinction between them. But our Greenwich Point residents are rabbits, not hares. Although they look alike at first glance, there is a considerable difference. Hares are slightly larger, with longer ears. The two species have different teeth. Hares are born precocial, with fur and open eyes; they can hop about soon after birth. Rabbits are altricial, i.e., naked, blind, and helpless for days after birth. Hares and rabbits do not cross-breed, and keep apart from each other; when hares were introduced onto the Isle of Man in the late eighteenth century, the more numerous resident rabbits ganged up on them and drove them off the island.

But both species breed, as the saying goes, like rabbits. As with so many animals (and birds), the buck rabbit stakes out his territory and awaits a female visitor. But unlike most mammals, the rabbit marks his boundaries with musk rather than urine. Both sexes secrete a yellowish glandular ooze through a row of pores under the chin; the buck's gland is the more active, especially as the mating season approaches, late in the winter. He hops about the area, rubbing his chin on the rocks and bushes until he has marked out the limits of his territory.

Often his first visitor is another male, which is promptly attacked. Buck dominance is usually established quickly, with the defender or invader driving the other away. But sometimes it can become a pitched battle until one or the other is bloodied and beaten. And when a female rabbit approaches the territory, the victorious buck makes a run at her also. In this case, however, he is merely showing off.

If he is fortunate, she is willing. A few females ready for mating even take the initiative, sexually harassing a male with ear-nibbling, nudging, and even mounting. But if the female is unwilling, the male can be very unfortunate. Female rabbits not ready for mating can defend themselves viciously; some would-be rabbit rapists have been partially castrated by angry females defending themselves.

When both are ready and willing, rabbit courtship, if that is the word, is usually a lively affair. When the buck makes a run at the doe, she may leap in the air. He may respond by leaping over her to show off his white belly. She may leap again while he runs under her. Then he propositions her in a unique fashion: He jumps over her again, this time spraying her back with his urine. This, zoologists say, marks her as his mate. It also, for reasons known only to rabbits, turns her on. Purring with pleasure, she squats on the ground and raises her posterior for him.

After the prolonged foreplay, the actual copulation is brief, taking only a few seconds. But the climax itself can be dramatic. At its conclusion the buck falls onto his side or back, as if suffering from cardiac arrest. Occasionally he will let go a piercing scream, which must be a bit unnerving for his mate. But within minutes he has recovered and is ready for more.

So is she, and they continue to mate for a day or so before separating, the female to go off and prepare for birth and the male to go looking for other conquests. There is some dispute about the sexual mores of rabbits. A few zoologists claim that they are generally monogamous. But most rabbits seem to disagree, feeling free to mate with every willing partner to come along. As naturalist J. G. Millais puts it, "On the whole, their morals are of the loosest description." An equally disapproving British couplet proclaims,

> They have such lost, degraded souls
> No wonder they inhabit holes.

The rabbit, of course, is quite unaware of such human disapprobation. There have even been instances of lesbian rabbit behavior, usually with females mounting each other; some have false pregnancies in which the female refuses all male advances and may even start to build a birthing nest. But most female rabbits prefer male rabbits, and homosexual male behavior is rare if it occurs at all.

The result is a lot of rabbits. A female can breed at as

young an age as four months. Her pregnancy usually lasts
less than a month. She is ready to mate again as soon as she
has given birth, and there is evidence that some females
have become pregnant again even before delivery. Most
females conceive again within twenty-four hours. With a
breeding season that starts in early spring and lasts until
autumn, an active, well-fed female can produce half a dozen
litters a year. Allowing for an average litter of five, one
female's progeny in a season is thirty rabbits; in four seasons she will bring forth 120.

Meanwhile, assuming that half of them are female, she
can become the nearly instant ancestor of more than two
thousand rabbits. Not to mention her male issue, all of
whom are hopping about fertilizing hundreds more females
during the same period. It is estimated that one male fathers
up to 180 rabbits per year. No wonder rabbits are regarded
in some parts of the world as symbols of fertility.

But in nature's continuing balancing act, the female
rabbit has a built-in method of abortion. Naturalists call it
resorption. Under the stress of crowded living conditions
and/or not enough to eat, the female's body absorbs the
fetuses, simultaneously nourishing her and curbing the local rabbit population.

Normally, however, the pregnancy proceeds quickly.
The female goes off on her own. In England, where the
rabbits burrow underground, she digs a tunnel branching
away from the rest of the warren and prepares her own
nursery, lining it with grass and her fur. Greenwich's cottontail simply hollows out a depression in the ground in
which she makes her birthing bed. Like the English rabbit,
she defends it from all intruders her size. Usually she selects
a site concealed by tall weeds or bushes. Sometimes she
makes her nest in a pile of leaves, sand, or detritus. Some

choose woodchuck holes, hollow stumps, or stone walls. One eccentric female's nest, containing five kits, was found in the crotch of a tree, ninety-five feet from the ground.

But some of our local rabbits can be casual about their nursery nests. Bicycling around the Point one day, I noticed a rabbit squatting on the ground at the edge of the road. Thinking it might be sick or wounded, I dismounted for a closer inspection, upon which she hopped away, revealing a newborn litter. I immediately retreated and watched from a distance until she returned.

Her kits scarcely resembled rabbits. They were amorphous little blobs of quivering grayish fuzz, blind and unable to move about. At first I feared the worst. I had read that a frightened mother might eat her young. (Sometimes she does, if starved for protein.) But this mother hovered over her brood for a few more days, and then they were gone. Baby rabbits grow fast because their mother's milk is extremely rich. (A nursing female drinks half a gallon of water a day.) The kits double their weight in a week. The litter may be as small as three or four, or as large as eight; if more than that, some of them starve because most female rabbits have only eight teats, and the runts of the litter lose out in the competition for their mother's milk.

By the second week their gray fur begins to turn brown, their eyes open, and they can hop about on their own. At three weeks they are nibbling at the grass around the nest, and are being weaned. After the first week or two, nursing is all the care they get, because their mother has already mated again and is preparing for her new litter. Beatrix Potter's idyllic rabbit household, with Peter, Flopsy, Mopsy, and Cottontail being brought up by their mother, is more myth than reality. Instead of being scolded for sneaking into Mr. MacGregor's garden, Peter in real life is on his own and already fathering more rabbits.

With the potential for such an exponential population explosion, why aren't we up to our armpits in rabbits? One answer is resorption, the rabbit's built-in abortion mechanism. Another is predators. Raccoons and rats, foxes and coyotes, weasels and snakes, owls and eagles, hawks and buzzards, dogs and cats all prey on the rabbit kits before they can be taught the art of survival.

Those that survive to maturity become experts at hiding death-still in their forms or blending into the underbrush; and they spend most of the daylight hours concealed. Their brownish fur makes excellent camouflage. (Most white pet rabbits, by the way, are inbred albinos.)

The rabbit also has bulging, extra-sensitive eyes that give it a 270-degree range of vision. Inside its nose are sensory pads that it can open to detect dangerous odors at considerable distances. Its large ears operate like radar dishes; each can turn independently to pick up the slightest warning noise.

Rabbits tend to feed in groups with lookouts whose loud thumping at the sign of danger sends all of them scampering. If cornered by a predator its size, a rabbit can use its razor-sharp teeth and claws and its powerful hind feet as effective weapons. And when attacked it can let out a bloodcurdling scream that warns every other rabbit within half a mile. But against large predators the rabbit's main defense is escape. One scared rabbit was clocked at more than forty miles an hour, covering ten feet at a leap. A rabbit on the run can employ maddening evasive action, then dart into hiding and freeze as its pursuer dashes by.

But predators are only one of the rabbit's perils. Quick as they are, many fail to make it across a highway. Deep snow can trap a rabbit and make it an easy target for a larger animal. Rabbits are infested with ticks, lice, tapeworms, bladderworms, and fleas; the last sometimes infects them with the rabbit's greatest nemesis, myxomatosis, which is almost always fatal. (Ticks and mosquitoes can also carry this disease.) They can catch cold, sniffling, sneezing, coughing, sometimes lapsing into pneumonia, which is often as deadly as myxomatosis. Sociable creatures, rabbits enjoy rubbing noses, thereby spreading infection through an entire group, especially in the underground warrens of the English species. Another deadly rabbit disease, particularly in the warrens, is coccidiosis, which is spread by rabbit feces. Grown rabbits have usually developed an immunity to this disease but are still carriers; one rabbit can pass as many as 55,000 parasite eggs in a day.

What with predators and diseases, only about a quarter of a female rabbit's litter may reach the age of two, their brown fur gradually turning gray. Few rabbits in the wild live more than three years. A pet rabbit, coddled in captivity, can reach the old age of twelve.

The rabbits in our neighborhood could hardly be called coddled, but they aren't very wild, either. Suburbanization has driven away many of their predators. Developers have turned forests into the fields that the rabbits prefer. And suburbanites have planted hedges that rabbits can hide in, as well as hundreds of juicy gardens in which they clearly enjoy foraging. As herbivores, they can survive on wild grasses, dandelions (they can have all they want of mine), clover, and berries. But no rabbit is stupid enough to pass up the lettuce, spinach, peas, beans, and carrots that we have carefully arranged for them in orderly rows. Fences, I found, rarely keep them out. Our rabbits may not burrow as deeply as their British cousins do, but they can dig under most fences; and a fenced-in rabbit will eat a lot more than will one just passing through.

Rabbits do not hibernate; during the winter I've seen them dig down through a few inches of snow to get at whatever green stems are left. The rabbit's two sets of teeth are perfectly adapted to a herbivorous life. The front set of long, sharp teeth neatly clip off the toughest plant; and the row of strong, flat molars in the back of the jaw quickly grind it to a pulp. The rabbit, I have read, also has a unique adaptation: a cavity in the mouth for temporarily storing its food. In fact, the rabbit has an intriguing, if not particularly attractive, eating habit to help it survive in the wild.

At first I assumed that our rabbits spent an inordinate amount of time grooming between their hind legs. Consulting the rabbit books, I found the answer, and was struck by a similarity to the whitetail deer.

Watching our rabbits foraging at dawn or dusk, I noticed that they generally covered a fairly large area, rarely lingering in one spot even when presented with a row of carrots. Evidently this maneuver is designed to provide an elusive target for predators. And every minute or so the rabbit stands on its hind legs, looks about, wrinkles its sensitive nose, and turns its ears to detect any intruder. Meanwhile it chomps, grinds, and swallows its food, as well as storing some in its mouth cavity. Shortly, as dawn turns to morning, it hops away to its hollowed-out form to lie low for the rest of the day, and the unique digestive process goes to work.

The zoologists call it *refection*. The masticated food bypasses the digestive juices of the intestine and emerges from the anus in the form of soft pellets. In what I took to be grooming, the rabbit leans over and gobbles up these pellets of undigested food, which it chews and swallows again. This time it is thoroughly digested and the waste is excreted in the hard, gray pellets we know as rabbit droppings. Thus, much like the ruminant deer, the rabbit is able to eat and run, to grab its food and go into hiding, where it can digest its meal in comparative safety.

Rabbits do spend a good deal of time actually grooming. From spring through summer they continue to molt, the winter fur giving way to a thinner summer coat, which in turn is replaced in the fall by heavier fur. (Rabbit molt is a boon to the local birds, who collect it from the bushes to line their nests.) The fur is waterproof; I have seen rabbits grazing in the rain, pausing frequently to shake like wet dogs. But unlike a dog, a rabbit cannot walk. Only its forelegs can move independently; its hind legs move together, so even while grazing a rabbit always hops.

Those forelegs are superb digging tools. European rabbits use them to make their mazes of tunnels; usually the females do the work, digging the passages and escape hatches for an entire colony. Around the warren are the rabbit latrines; they are careful always to go outside to leave their droppings. Since one rabbit can let go about 360 of these pellets daily, zoologists often count them to estimate the population of the colony. The rabbits sometimes use the latrines to mark their boundaries; the smell is enough to warn off invaders. But it was not enough to deter some puffins on an island off England who appropriated a rabbit colony's tunnels, forcing out the residents to be devoured by the island's huge gulls.

European rabbits generally prefer a loose, sandy soil, which they often honeycomb with so many tunnels that it collapses under the weight of larger animals. Unwary predators can become trapped in one of these burrows. A few years ago, Miss Pepper, a border terrier belonging to Queen Beatrix of the Netherlands, unwisely poked her nose into a rabbit burrow at the queen's residence in The Hague, got stuck, and suffocated. The queen, her court announced, was "deeply upset" and officially banned rabbits from the royal residence.

As every child knows, Alice entered one of these rabbit wonderlands when she followed one down his hole. Alice's creator, Lewis Carroll, was no doubt inspired by the veritable hierarchy established by British rabbits in their underground warrens. One such warren can house as many as thirty rabbits, including a dominant male, a few subservient males, and a covey of females. As more rabbits are born and mature, the warren becomes crowded and the weaker members of the colony are forced out. They then dig a new warren, where they proceed to set up their own hierarchical colony.

But unlike the rabbits of, say, Greenwich, England, the rabbits of Greenwich, Connecticut, are content to live aboveground. And American suburbanites have conveniently provided them with the cleared fields, hedges, and stone walls—not to mention the vegetable gardens—that rabbits particularly like. Apparently the bushes, flower gardens, and frequently mowed fields of Greenwich Point satisfy most of its rabbit population, because our nearby garden is relatively rabbit-free. And the occasional invasion is a mixed menace because rabbit pellets make excellent fertilizer, having a highly nutritious 2 percent nitrogen content, more than that of most animal manures. Rabbit droppings make useful additions to the compost pile (though we discovered that too many can give it an unattractive odor). And the pellets can be ground up, bagged, and saved for future use.

My friends farther inland, however, are less receptive. Rabbits regularly devour their vegetables and fruits at the first sprigs of green. During the ensuing summer the gardeners and rabbits contend for the growing plants. Even during the winter the rabbits continue to plague them, usually by chewing the roots, bark, and twigs of shrubs and such trees as birch and maple, often ringing the trunks and killing the smaller trees.

In some areas of the United States during the earlier part of this century, the human victims reacted with the typical human response of slaughtering them. Rabbit-hunting became a highly acclaimed sport until the inevitable backlash from animal-lovers—especially, I remember, when *Life* magazine published some brutal photographs of townspeople in Ohio rounding up rabbits so the children could have the pleasure of clubbing them to death.

Elsewhere in the world, rabbit paranoia led to even more lethal measures. British property owners felt particularly victimized by the destruction of their crops; one was reported to have committed suicide, his last words being

"Rabbits have ruined me!" With characteristic dedication, British landlords raised rabbit-hunting to mass massacre. The Prince of Wales (before becoming Edward VII) purchased the royal home of Sandringham in 1863 chiefly for the sport, and promptly raised the annual game bag from seven thousand to thirty thousand. Two years earlier, Lord Stamford, on his Bradgate Park estate in Leicestershire, set something of a record by mowing down 3,333 rabbits with only thirteen guns in a single day.

Britons also employed a variety of imaginative methods of rabbit depredation, some of which proved counterproductive. Soaking crops with rum or brandy and clubbing the drunken foragers turned out to be too expensive. Steeping vegetables in arsenic not only poisoned other animals but also ran the risk of affecting humans. Pumping cyanide into the rabbit warrens was also dangerously indiscriminate. More effective was the use of trained ferrets to invade warrens and drive the rabbits into snare nets staked at the exits.

But the British rabbits survived. One inevitable result of the popularity of rabbit hunting, for example, was a proliferation of areas set aside to breed more rabbits for sportsmen, thereby helping offset the population decline. Then, with the perfection of the shotgun, English sportsmen turned their deadly attention to pheasants, partridges, and grouse, exterminating most of these birds' carnivorous predators so as to protect the birds for their shooting parties. Since most of the birds' predators—foxes, weasels, badgers, and raptors—were also the rabbits' predators, the rabbit began to flourish again throughout England.

In France, landowners tried cyanide and sulfur cartridges in the warrens. And as in England, rabbit hunting became popular as well as fashionable. In what seems a fitting irony, the self-professed amatory predator Casanova de Seingalt complained in his memoirs that one of his targets of seduction did not keep an assignation with him, opting instead for an afternoon of rabbit-hunting with a French nobleman.

The most brutal method of curbing the rabbit population was the introduction of myxomatosis. Caused by a virus transmitted by biting insects, it was discovered in Uruguay, whose rabbits had developed an immunity to it. When two European rabbits were experimentally infected and loosed in France in the 1950s, the disease spread with astonishing rapidity. Only a year later it was recorded in England, where it infected the local rabbit population with equal speeed.

Myxomatosis does its work in only a few days, causing swelling of the eyes and ears until the rabbit is nearly blind and deaf and becomes disoriented, an easy prey to predators, who seem not to be affected. A national outcry against the disease as a form of rabbit control led in only two years to its being outlawed in England. Even then it was almost too late. Passed by infected rabbits in multiplying numbers, myxomatosis killed nearly 90 percent of England's rabbit population in only five years. So many rabbit corpses littered the English countryside that the army had to be called out to remove them as a health hazard. Britain's rabbit population today, as a result, is only a minor problem. Some British rabbits seem to have developed a partial immunity, but periodic outbreaks still occur. Perhaps as an adaptation, many British rabbits, like our American cottontails, have given up burrowing and live and breed on the surface where the virus-carrying fleas, ticks, and other insects are not so prevalent.

The most famous (or infamous) introduction of myxomatosis was in Australia, where by the mid-twentieth century rabbits appeared to be overrunning the continent.

Australians first tried a unique method of population control. In a selected area, all the rabbits were routed out but only the females were killed—the theory being that the overwhelming numbers of males would wear out the few remaining females. But the word evidently spread through the rabbit network, because hundreds of neighboring females rushed in to take advantage of the abundance of males, and the numbers of rabbits increased even more. So the Australians resorted to myxomatosis, and shortly the rabbits were dying by the millions. Today the continent's rabbit population seems to have stabilized, largely because most Australian rabbits have built up a resistance to the disease.

In what might be called a rabbit paradox, while environmentalists are struggling to control the rabbit population, farmers in many parts of the world are growing them. Rabbits make excellent laboratory animals. Despite a mounting outcry from animal-rights groups, rabbits are used to test the toxicity of cosmetics and nicotine because their reactions so resemble those of humans. Rabbits are also bred to feed zoo animals, rabbit meat being highly nutritious. Hospitals make use of rabbit meat because it is more easily digested by patients with ulcers and other stomach disorders. Although rabbit was once a staple of many restaurant menus, its popularity has declined in the latter part of this century. In England, for example, rabbit meat was shunned because of myxomatosis, despite assurances from zoologists that the disease cannot be transmitted to humans. In France, rabbit is still a regular item on most restaurant menus and in meat markets, further proving that the French either are smarter or will eat anything.

So the rabbit, an attractive feature of the landscape, a boon to the compost pile, and withal an endearing little critter, provides in this ultimate sacrifice a nutritious and delicious gift to mankind. Rabbits can be fried, barbecued, or made into dumplings, salad, casseroles, stews, and biscuit pies. And meanwhile, millions of other rabbits are out there, making sure that there will be plenty more where these came from.

NINE

Bats in the Attic

WE were sitting on my friend's porch at dusk when something suddenly shot above the horizon, flashed to right and left, and streaked past us at what seemed the speed of light.

"What kind of bird," I asked my friend, "was *that*?"

"That," said my friend, "was no bird. That was a bat."

I then remembered seeing one a few days earlier. Our friend had converted his barn into a summer home and had rented it to us for the season. In the hollow of an exposed beam, my wife had spotted what looked like a suspended mouse. Realizing that it was a bat, we had panicked as most humans do. It would, we were sure, cover our floor with guano; it would fly into my wife's hair; it would bite us and give us rabies; it might even suck out all our blood. We had kept our distance and left the door open; shortly the bat had whisked out; we had slammed the door; and, to our great relief, it had not returned.

Now, watching the incredible speed and grace of what may have been our former visitor, I began to think again about bats. Partly with the guidance of my friend, who took a benign view of all creatures, even snakes and bats, I did some amateur research on these little critters. And when I consulted some of the many books on the subject,

I found that most zoologists had concluded that the bat was much maligned.

The sources inevitably led me to Dr. Merlin D. Tuttle, who is world-renowned as the bats' best friend. Dr. Tuttle's organization, Bat Conservation International, has more than twelve thousand members in fifty-five countries who regard him as their guru. Their mantra is that the bat, far from being a menace, is one of nature's great benefactors. While visiting a friend in Texas, my wife and I paid a visit to BCI's headquarters, where we found Dr. Tuttle so persuasive that I, too, became convinced that the bats have had a bum rap. And now, in our own home, I am trying to attract them.

Bats, I have discovered, are not evil, dirty, blind little beasts of moonlit nights, associated with witches and other ominous agents of the devil. Certainly they are not dirty; most of them are far tidier than birds, spending a great deal of their time licking, cleaning, and grooming themselves. They are content to suspend themselves on perches to sleep, unlike birds that build verminous nests. Despite the popular epithet "blind as a bat," all bats can see, and some have excellent vision. Despite their reputation as flying werewolves at the full moon, bats tend to stay home on their perches during moonlit nights. Nor do they deliberately fly into anyone's hair; they are far too adept on the wing even to do so by accident. In fact, Dr. Tuttle tested the theory by putting a bat in a woman's hair; it slipped off her head, rescuing itself only by grabbing a trailing strand. (The myth evidently originated in the early days when few houses had ceilings and newborn bats, still unable to fly, lost their hold on a roof beam.)

Nor do bats spread disease as much as other animals do. Some bats are carriers of, and suffer from, histoplasmosis, a fungus that can cause lung disease. But rarely has a human contacted histoplasmosis from bats; much more often the carrier is a pigeon or a chicken. Bats infected with rabies have been found in most states of the United States, but Dr. Denny Constantine, an acknowledged authority on bat diseases, claims that a rabid bat will usually sicken and die quickly, almost never attacking another animal. Rabid foxes, raccoons, skunks, cats, and dogs infect far more humans.

As for the dreaded vampire bat, there are only three species, confined to parts of Central and South America; and they prefer livestock to humans. Bat defenders even claim that some bats are attractive (well, at least cute). A few resemble miniature puppies; some have rabbit ears. But even the most ardent bat fancier has to admit that some of the more grotesque hog-nosed, distorted, spiked, fang-baring specimens can only be called ugly by normal aesthetic standards.

It is partly because of the bat's appearance that zoologists have had such a hard time overcoming what would technically be called chiropterophobia—a hatred of bats. (Count Dracula, of course, did not help.) Dr. Tuttle recounts a case of a workman at a TVA dam who claimed that bats had mauled his arm when he had reached into his locker. Every other workman refused to enter the locker room—until Tuttle demonstrated that the teeth of the local bats were much too small to inflict such lacerations and that a jagged edge of the locker had caused the wound; by that time a panicked doctor was already giving the workman rabies shots. Tuttle claims that unnecessarily terrified chiropterophobes have broken legs and nearly drowned trying to escape presumed attacks; and he recalls one instance in which overzealous fumigation to rid a house of bats burned it down.

Far from being the menace they are reputed to be,

bats are highly beneficial to man. They consume enormous amounts of insects and other pests. The little brown bat, common throughout the United States, can gobble up 150 mosquitoes in fifteen minutes. (And the *Anopheles* mosquito is a greater disease carrier than the bat.) Some insect-eating bats consume 25 percent of their body weight in bugs in half an hour. Scientists have calculated that the millions of Mexican free-tailed bats (so called because their tails extend beyond the tail membrane) that spend their summers in Texas put away more than six thousand *tons* of insects during the season. Some species of bats also eat cockroaches, mice, termites, Japanese beetles, potato beetles, corn borers, ants, caterpillars, moths, and even scorpions. (Other species eat fruit, fish, frogs, birds, and other bats. One frog-eating species has even learned how to imitate the frog's call.) Fortunately, most bats, which preferred caves and trees before civilization began to intrude on their habitats, have adapted by moving into attics and barns, bridges and towers. Zoologist Charles A. R. Campbell urges homeowners to hang bat houses near their birdhouses for mosquito control. Bat houses (which resemble birdhouses without a floor) have been popular in Europe and Australia for half a century and are just now becoming popular in the United States.

BCI has encouraged many thousands of home owners to erect bat houses, one of which I dutifully hung on the side of our house. Dr. Tuttle had told me that while a survey had shown that 83 percent of their official bat houses, when properly installed, had attracted the little critters, I should not expect mine to be occupied immediately; it might not be discovered by our local bats for a year or so. Nonetheless, I happily noticed that the mosquito population near the bat house nearly disappeared that summer. Clearly the mere sight of the bat house persuaded the mosquitoes to get out while they still could. (A zoologist friend considers this an unscientific conclusion, but it seems to me a simple case of cause and effect.)

As if not content to rid the community of pests, the bat converts them into a most useful substance. Bat guano, one of the best natural fertilizers, has been mined commercially from many caves and caverns; more than 100,000 tons of it were dug out of Carlsbad Cavern in the first forty years of this century. In advocating bat houses, Dr. Campbell points out that they can also provide fertilizer for the garden. I'm looking forward to that.

Bats also cross-pollinate such flowers and trees as banana and breadfruit, avocado, mango, and guava. And like flying Johnny Appleseeds, they propagate vegetation far and wide, spitting out inedible seeds or eliminating them with the rich fertilizer of their droppings. It is estimated that two dozen genera of tropical trees and flowers are propagated by bat droppings. A fruit bat can spread as many as sixty thousand seeds abroad in a single night. The baobab, Africa's "tree of life," depends on bats to distribute its seeds. So do Africa's iroko tree, the basis of a timber industry worth millions, and the durian fruit trees of Southeast Asia, which produce some $120 million worth of fruit annually. One BCI study indicated that more than three hundred tropical plant species depend on bats to propagate their seeds.

In one of the many wonders of nature's adaptation, some plants (called "bat flowers") have evolved especially to foster propagation by bats. Unlike most flowers, they close by day and open at night when birds and bees are asleep and bats are active. Many of these plants grow high up on tree branches or vines, where the bats can sample them on the wing. Some have developed odors particularly attractive to bats; one of the flowers has long, bushy stamens to smear pollen on the body of the bat as it sips the plant's nectar.

In some parts of the world, larger bats provide food for humans. African markets sell bats as big as quail; some Africans consider bat fat a cure for rheumatism and baldness. In Thailand, huge two-pound fruit-eating bats sell for three bahts per bat (one baht equals about fifteen cents); some Thais believe that bat blood diluted with whiskey is a powerful aphrodisiac—as well as a treatment for the backache that might ensue. Java and the Philippines have large bats that subsist on fruit and taste like pork. Borneo natives enjoy bat pies. And a cookbook author in Australia, Mrs. Lance Rawson, has published a recipe for bat pie: "I cut them up, along with an onion, and seasoned with all sorts of herbs, and stewed them for a couple of hours, then turned them into a pie dish and covered with a good paste." She claims they taste like suckling pig.

But what struck me most was that beyond its beneficial qualities, zoologists have discovered that the bat—classed as the order Chiroptera (*chiro* is greek for "hand," and *ptera* for "wing")—is one of the world's most fascinating critters. There are bats that fly openmouthed through insect swarms, gobbling them up like whales swimming through krill. There are long-legged, sharp-clawed fishing bats that swoop like hawks to gaff their prey (and can often be heard crunching their catch as they fly away). There are bats with anteaterlike tongues and tubular nostrils that serve as snorkels when they bury their heads in ripe fruit. There are pink, hairless bats with special pouches for their folded wings. There are bats with suction cups on their wrists and ankles to cling to smooth surfaces; when plucked away, their suckers pop like wine corks. There are female bats that form their own chastity belts. There are wasp-sized bats that weigh less than a matchbook and are the smallest mammals in the world; there are super-bats called flying foxes with six-foot wingspans. And there was a Mexican free-tailed bat that starred in a movie.

There are a lot of bats on the planet, at least 850 species, almost one-fourth of all animal species; bats are the largest order of mammals excepting only rodents. North America is home to only about forty of all these bat species, but some of the larger caves in the Southwest swarm with millions of them. Bracken Cave, near San Antonio, Texas, one fifth of a mile long and about 60 feet wide, shelters some 20 million Mexican free-tailed bats, the largest aggregation of mammals anywhere in the world—all of them hanging by their toes.

One of nature's awe-inspiring spectacles is the sight of these millions of bats swirling from the cave like smoke, rising in massive, counterclockwise-wheeling clouds to some ten thousand feet to catch a tailwind before taking off for their feeding grounds, many miles away. They will complete a journey of thousands of square miles before returning at dawn, when they dive into the cave in another black cloud to hang themselves up and sleep until dusk.

Bat fossils found in Wyoming and in Messel, Germany, are more than 50 million years old. And they have evolved into a bewildering variety of species. There are naked bats and woolly bats; Old World bats and New World bats; ghost bats and tomb bats; bulldog, butterfly, and horseshoe bats; dawn bats and harpy bats; red, black, and blue bats; mouse-eared bats and mouse-tailed bats; short-tailed, free-tailed, and sheath-tailed bats; bare-backed bats and naked-backed mustached bats; tube-nosed, leaf-nosed, and plain-nosed bats; club-footed and sucker-footed bats; hammerhead, flat-headed, slit-faced, funnel-eared, disc-winged, and thumbless bats.

Bats are the only mammals that fly. Unrelated to birds

(which of course are not mammals, laying eggs instead of bearing their young live), most bats fly more slowly on the straightaway but are far more agile. Some bats can hover like a hummingbird, others can soar like an eagle, most can dart about better than any bird. The fastest species is the big brown bat, which has been clocked at more than thirty miles an hour. (A bat that flew right past a helicopter going forty miles an hour was probably helped by a tailwind; or perhaps it was the original "bat out of hell.") In one study, a female long-eared bat managed to take off hefting 73 percent of her own weight.

Indeed, the bat's wing is one of nature's marvels. A thin but strong membrane stretching from forearms to ankles, it makes the bat resemble a mouse with a cape— thus in German it is called *Fledermaus* and in Spanish *ratón volador* (flying mouse). And, of course, it is the cape that distinguishes the American comic-book hero Batman. The bat's wings not only help it outmaneuver every other flying creature; they also aid in snaring its food; swooping down on an insect, the bat can scoop it out of the air in a canopy formed by curling up the end joints of its wings. The bat also uses its wings to put on courtship displays and to cool off by fanning itself and by releasing heat through its thin wing membrane in a radiator effect.

It is partly because of the bat's wings that it perches head downward; most of its upper limbs form part of the wings. And the bat's legs and feet are wonderfully adapted to this position, with tendons that lock in place so the bat's toes will not let go while it sleeps. The bat can hang by one foot while stuffing food into its mouth with the other. The bat's heart is comparatively large for a mammal, and amazingly strong. During flight it can pump blood at 1,300 beats per minute, compared to two hundred while at rest.

There are bats on every continent except Antarctica;

in the Americas they range from the Arctic Circle to the southern tip of South America. In the cooler temperate zones of the United States, some insect-eating bats whose food disappears in the fall migrate like birds. They cannot match the annual odyssey of some birds—the Arctic tern's flight nearly from pole to pole, for example—but bats banded in some Kentucky caves were recaptured 350 miles to the north, in Indiana, Ohio, and Michigan; some were found back in Kentucky after their return. Mexican free-tailed bats migrate nearly eight hundred miles to Texas every spring, returning every fall. No one has yet figured out how they do it, though some experiments have demonstrated the bat's extraordinary memory for its neighborhood. Foraging guano bats cruise as far as fifty miles from their roosts each night. And zoologists have found magnetic substances in bats' brains, indicating some connection to the two poles.

Most bats also have a highly developed homing instinct. In one test, three big brown bats returned to their roost when released 450 miles away. A couple in Toledo, Ohio, fed mealworms to a bat that made its home on a beam over their patio. When it became ill, they took it to the zoo five miles away, where it recovered and was set free for its winter migration. But first it returned to its patio perch to check in before heading south. By spring it was back again at the same perch.

For a while some scientists were puzzled by a group of supposedly intelligent, not to say lazy, little brown bats that seemed to be traveling as stowaways. On every voyage, sailors aboard the ship *Avon Forest*, which made a regular run to Europe from Dalhousie, Canada, found bats emerging from the vessel at their destination. Zoologist Brock Fenton provided a relatively mundane solution to the mystery. The bats used the dock area for their feeding flights, occasionally resting aboard the *Avon Forest* and, perhaps to their surprise as well, eventually finding themselves in Southampton or Rotterdam.

Some bats of the northern regions do not migrate, but hibernate until the insects return in the spring. They usually retreat to a cave far enough underground for the temperature to remain above the freezing point. One species wraps itself in its wings for added warmth. Most hibernating bats go into such a deep torpor that they appear dead. Their heartbeat is imperceptible, their body temperature is close to freezing, and they scarcely breathe. A few can remain in this state for up to six months, subsisting on body fat they have stored up during the previous summer; some of these fat bats are as much as 50 percent overweight at the start of hibernation. Occasionally a hibernating bat will rouse, grumble, empty its bladder, and go back to sleep.

Most bats go into near hibernation every day in a deep sleep, hanging upside down in rows like so many dead leaves until they wake at dusk for another night of flying and feeding. Because they fly by night and roost in the dark by day, they are black, gray, or brown, and color-blind; they have no need for colorful displays like those of daytime birds.

Bats will roost in any comparatively dark place: attics, caves, barns, hollow trees, culverts, the undersides of bridges. When the Congress Avenue Bridge in Austin, Texas, was rebuilt some years ago, the new design included grooves on the underside that provided perfect perches for bats. Residents were at first alarmed when nearly a million Mexican free-tails promptly moved in. Local newspapers ran scare headlines like MASS FEAR IN THE AIR AS BATS INVADE AUSTIN. Dr. Tuttle, who had just moved his office to Austin, persuaded the mayor to install near the bridge an educational exhibit on the benefits of bats. Soon the menace became a tourist attraction; and today in August, when the bridge's bat population is at its height, thousands of people gather to watch the evening outpouring, and it is difficult to get a dinner reservation at the nearby restaurants. Meanwhile the bats consume an estimated fourteen *tons* of local insects every night.

Contrary to legend, there are usually more birds than bats in church belfreys. One of our Greenwich churches attracted a few hundred bats, not to the belfrey but to the organ pipes, which make excellent bat roosts. The parishioners were startled to see a cloud of bats erupt at the first peal of the organ—though not so startled, of course, as the bats, who nonetheless returned after each service. When their droppings soiled the pews, the church wardens had to drape them with removable cloths (after some discussion over whether or not the cloth had to be consecrated). The bats remained until an exterminator succeeded in making the church much less of a bat sanctuary, and the unwelcome visitors reluctantly departed.

This treatment was more humane than that of an eccentric lady I was told about who, some years ago, conceived a unique and draconian method of ridding her attic of bats. Attics are ideal locations for bats, especially mothers-to-be looking for a dark, raftered, and warm nursery. As her granddaughter tells it, this woman and her children would periodically don bathing caps to protect their hair, climb into the unlit attic at dusk, and run about slashing away with old tennis racquets, creating a veritable bat massacre. Dr. Tuttle, who would most emphatically disapprove of this method of bat control, says that the best way to keep bats out of the attic is to seal up all the crevices through which they can get in. But the tennis racquet method, I'm told, was equally effective.

Not all bat species require total darkness for their daytime sleep. Some fruit bats fashion their own tents, biting along the vein of a banana leaf so it droops to provide shade and protection from the rain. One eastern horseshoe bat in Australia's Lake Eacham National Park was found roosting on a beam in a men's room, soiling with its droppings a toilet seat that someone had forgotten to leave up.

The inhabitants of bat roosts can number from one or two to millions. So many bats roost in a cave near the end of a runway of Randolph Air Force Base in Texas that air-traffic controllers can see their swarms on radar and schedule airplane takeoffs and landings to avoid their evening departures and morning arrivals.

The nightly outpourings are spectacular. One zoologist studying a colony watched them erupt at dusk in a black cloud visible for two miles; in twenty minutes he calculated that nearly 9 million bats had poured out for their nightly feeding foray.

They are marvelously adapted to their diet. Many insect-eating bats have especially sharp teeth that churn an insect's hard exoskeleton into mush with the speed of a Cuisinart. Others that cannot chomp so fast have cheek pouches for storing food to chew later on the perch. Some fruit-eating bats not only have tongues a third of their body length, but also mouths capable of separating the digestible pulp from the indigestible seeds and skins, which they wad into pellets and spit out. Large carnivorous bats swoop through the forest at night, picking off birds and rats from the branches and carrying them back to their roosts to eat at leisure. Unlike birds, which have to tip up their heads to swallow water, a bat can skim across a pond, lapping up a drink with its tongue.

The three vampire species that help give the bat a bad name were discovered by Columbus when he landed in Trinidad in 1498. The vampire is a true specialist, with one

set of razor-edged teeth to shave off a victim's fur and a lancetlike set to make a quick, shallow incision while dripping an anticoagulant into the wound. Vampires, unlike most other bats, are nimble on the ground and can creep up on a horse or cow to nip it in the leg and lap up the blood. Vampires prefer sleeping prey, and their bite is usually so painless that the victim doesn't even wake. Although the vampire rarely attacks people, legends of human victims abound; in a movie made from the book *Papillon*, about Devil's Island, the director, unable to locate a true vampire, had to settle for an innocent Mexican free-tailed bat.

Returning with full stomachs near dawn, the bats

crowd into their roost, bickering and squealing as they vie
for perch space and adding their droppings to the accumula-
tion of guano on the cave floor. Although most bats have
a sense of smell, they seem to be impervious to the strong
stench of guano, whose high ammonia content can snuff
out the flame of a lantern. Zoologists doing research in
these caves must wear respirators. Bat experts D. W. Yalden and P. A. Morris described a typical bat roost in the
Tamana Cave of central Trinidad, with its "thick porridge"
of guano steaming in the humid, nearly one-hundred-degree
temperatures, supporting a vast variety of beetles and giant
cockroaches, which in turn fed invading toads and land
crabs, snakes and opossums, the Dantesque scene buzzing
with flies. "The whole Tamana Cave," they wrote, "is a
seething, heaving mass of life in total darkness and a Turk-
ish-bath atmosphere. Biologically it is fascinating, but from
all other viewpoints utterly revolting!"

In most such colonies the male and female bats keep
apart. The sex life of the bat is normally promiscuous.
At breeding time, usually in the autumn, male bats will
frequently hover near a cave entrance, pouncing on every
female they can catch. But the usual procedure is for female
bats to go looking for suitable males, which emit *kwoking*
sounds to attract them and in some species perform courtship flights to demonstrate their agility and/or engage in
mock battles with other males. Some male bats are successful enough to establish harems, though females appear to
move at will from one harem to another.

A few species take the time for a bit of nuzzling, but
most bats mate unceremoniously. (Male bats have comparatively the largest reproductive organs of all mammals,
which has led some peoples to regard the bat as a symbol of
fertility.) Once impregnated, the female retires to a nursing
colony and has nothing more to do with the father of her

young; he never knows, or seems to care, which of the new generation is his.

One of the wonders of bat reproduction is what zoologists call "sperm storage," a mechanism found in few mammals. A newborn bat has a better chance to survive its first year, which is the most perilous, if it is born in early spring, allowing time for it to store up fat for winter hibernation or gain strength for migration. And since mating usually occurs in the fall, the female bat stores the implanted sperm through her hibernation period. She does not use this private sperm bank until early the following spring, when her ovulation and pregnancy begin. In addition, during hibernation many females form a vaginal "plug" to prevent further mating and protect the sperm they already carry.

Pregnant females usually retire to their nurseries in the caves earlier than the males, who continue mate-hunting for a few more weeks until most of the females are impregnated; then they retire to their bachelor quarters for hibernation. By early spring, when the now-ovulating females end their hibernation, the males are still sleeping it off. So, as Dr. Tuttle points out, the pregnant females, who need to consume their weight in insects every night, have a few critical weeks of feeding on all those spring bugs before having to compete with the males.

After a pregnancy varying from forty days to nine months (in the largest bats), the mother hooks her feet and wings to the perch so that her wings form a canopy to catch the baby. Some mothers-to-be even hang in an upright position so that gravity can assist the delivery. The bat's labor takes up to half an hour, and her birthing cries are ignored by the other females around her. The baby usually emerges rump-first to protect its tender, barely developed wings.

It is comparatively large, up to one-third of its

mother's weight (the equivalent of a forty-pound human baby). It arrives pink, naked, blind—only during its first week is a bat truly blind—and already screaming. As soon as its mother has cut its umbilical cord, it scrambles up to grab hold of her fur with tooth and claw. Some mothers carry their newborn on their backs for a few days. But most insect-eating species, because of their aerial acrobatics, soon leave their young behind while on the hunt; the babies emit a continuous squeal until their mothers' return. The arriving mother can pick out the call and scent of her own infant amid the bedlam of hundreds of thousands of screeching youngsters. But while their mothers are out foraging, many baby bats fall from their perches to the cave floor, where waiting beetles and cockroaches reduce them to skeletons in a matter of minutes. At least half of the young bats do not survive their first year.

A young bat learns to fly in about four weeks. Its first solo must be a breathtaking experience for the youngster, dropping from its perch, darting about at twenty feet per second in the darkness of a cave crowded with thousands of other first-time fliers, then somersaulting to land back on the cave wall. If it crash-lands, its mother dives down to coax it back into the air. About five weeks later the youngster is weaned and already learning the intricate business of catching its own dinner on the wing.

More like humans than like most other mammals, bats generally have one offspring; only a few rare species have twins, triplets, or quadruplets. But despite their low birth rate, they preserve their large population by longevity and many breeding seasons. An average bat lifespan is ten to fifteen years; some have lived more than twenty. Two little brown bats, already adults when banded in an Ontario mine in the late 1940s, were recaptured in 1979, more than thirty years old, still hale and hearty and presumably still breeding. As one zoologist put it, "You're talking about little bitty creatures with the lifespan of a black bear." Birds, in contrast, produce clutches of eggs but live for only a few years.

Of all the marvels of bat lore, nothing is so remarkable as the way it can fly in the dark. Until recent years this was one of the great mysteries of animal behavior. How could these fast-flying creatures dart about through total darkness, avoiding every obstacle in their paths?

As early as the eighteenth century, zoologist Lazarro Spallanzini found that bats did not possess an acute form of night sight, as had been believed. Nocturnal barn owls, for example, have highly developed light-sensitive eyes for night flying. But they frequently blunder into walls in total darkness. Bats, however, chase down insects they cannot see. Spallanzini and other experimenters tried temporarily blinding bats and found that their flight was unimpeded. But when the bats' ears were blocked, they were far less efficient.

What were they listening to? The zoologists could hear bats communicating with one another in squeaks and growls, but what could the bats hear as they approached and nimbly avoided the wires that the experimenters put in their path in darkened rooms? And how did they home in on flying insects that seemed to make no noise at all?

The answer did not come until research began into ultrasound, noises beyond the pitch of the human ear. Only in the 1940s, when a Harvard undergraduate, Donald Griffin, took some captive bats to a laboratory with ultrasound equipment did he find that the flying bat sends out signals unheard by humans and navigates by listening to echoes— a form of sonar perfected by the bat many eons before man began to use it. Griffin called it *echolocation*; and it is still more complex than man's sonar.

The flying bat emits a steady stream of ultrasonic noises from its larynx, its tongue, or its nostrils, depending on the species (which is why, to a human, a flying bat appears to be baring its teeth). The bat then computes how long it has taken the sound to reach an object in its path and be reflected back—indicating that bats figured out the speed of sound many centuries ago. Some of the knobs, spikes, spears, and other distortions that make a bat's face grotesque are receptors for this echolocation mechanism. The calculation is almost instantaneous: an object one yard away, for example, will echo the bat's sound in six one-thousands of a second, and the bat will record it and compute the location of the object in time to take evasive action.

This last-moment course change, Dr. Tuttle points out, is mistaken by many people for a bat attack; if they stand still, the bat will miss them, but usually they panic and duck into the bat just as it is veering away. The bat's echolocation is so sophisticated that it works even when the creature's mouth is full of prey; and it can detect not only the distance but also the size, shape, density, and even texture of the object. A flying bat will avoid a wire but pounce on a mosquito. One experimenter discovered that bats like soft-textured objects when his test subjects kept attacking a tennis ball.

The keenest human ear can detect a sound of about twenty thousand vibrations per second; bats send and receive up to two hundred thousand. Some bats can hear a bug burrowing in the sand or even a moth fluttering its wings. The bats send their signals at intervals of twenty to thirty times per second, pausing to listen for the echo. Faster and louder echoes tell the bat not only that it is approaching its prey, but also the insect's speed and direction. And as it closes in, it speeds up its signals to home in on its victim.

Even more impressive, the bat can use its echolocation on various levels, employing one wavelength of sound to avoid large objects and another to detect an insect—with what must be an occasionally embarrassing result when a bat chasing a bug smacks into a wall because it has turned off one part of its sonar to concentrate with another on its fleeing prey. Bats evidently avoid collisions with other bats not so much with echolocation as with regular squawks or growls. They have even learned that rain absorbs high-frequency sound, confusing their echolocation, so they tend to stay in their roosts on rainy days. (They also presumably know that a wet bat can catch a life-threatening cold.) As early an observer as Aristotle noticed that bats are good weather forecasters. When the bats stayed home, the night was likely to be stormy.

Echolocation even helps a fishing bat locate its prey. At first, after solving the mystery of the bat's sonic radar, scientists puzzled over how it could penetrate water. Observations finally showed that the fishing bat prefers calm water. Its echolocation is so delicate that it can detect the slightest ripple caused by a fish nearing the surface, and the bat dives unerringly onto the exact spot. Fish-eating bats have adapted to their specialty, developing short, greasy, waterproof fur, and learning to swim. But the bat has not yet solved one hazard of echolocation fishing: sometimes the ripples are made by a fish large enough to gobble up the bat.

In another example of nature's continuous adaptation, some insects—especially moths and lacewings—have developed sonar detectors. In BCI's publication *Bats*, zoologist James Fullard describes the aerial warfare of bats and moths in a debriefing better than anything we got during the Persian Gulf war. Some moths, Dr. Fullard writes, have an early-detection system that can pick up the echolocation of the big brown bat, one of its major predators, as much as one hundred feet away, long before the bat's sensitive sonar has spotted the moth. Ordinarily this is enough warning for the moth to escape. But in some circumstances—in a dense forest, for example—the bat's echolocation signals may be obscured or distorted. The bat, still undetected, now picks up the sounds of the moth, locks onto it, and switches to its attack wavelength or "feeding buzz."

The moth, however, has a backup system that detects this "sonar gunfire," as Dr. Fullard calls it. The prey, with the attacker virtually on its tail, immediately goes into "a series of wild, looping aerial maneuvers designed to outfly the heavier and less agile bat." Often these gyrations take the moth out of the bat's echolocation beam, and the bat gives up and goes looking for other prey. But if the bat is still locked onto the moth and closes in for the kill, the moth folds its wings and makes a desperate dive for the ground where the bat has a more difficult time locating it. The tiger moth even has one last defense, a blast of high-pitched clicks that in effect jams the bat's sonar while the tiger moth gets the hell out of there.

And just as weapons designers continue to refine their products, nature has evolved some Stealth bomber–like tropical bats whose echolocation is too high-pitched even for the moths. Others, whom the scientists call "whispering bats," use echolocation too faint for their victims to detect it. Attack and defense—this natural one-upmanship goes on in weapons systems far more sophisticated than those of man. One of the higher developments of hunting bats, for example, is that of the giant leaf-nosed bat, which doesn't waste its time chasing about after insects. It merely sits on a tree limb and waits for them to fly by; using its own variation of echolocation, it can track their flight path and intercept them with a minimum of effort.

Man has profited in countless ways from this highly sophisticated little animal. There may be small merit in the ancient beliefs that bats' hair and blood are nostrums for rheumatism and baldness, but modern science has gained a great deal from the study of bats. Its nearly transparent wings have helped with the microscopic examination of blood circulation—the effect of inhaled tobacco smoke on blood vessels, for example. Bats, which are assaulted by almost innumerable pests and diseases, have yielded antibodies for thirty-two viruses. The unique bacteria of bat guano are helping scientists improve detergents and detoxify industrial wastes. Radar and sonar technology have been enhanced by studying the bat's more intricate echolocation, and further study of the bat's tiny receptors may help miniaturize man's comparatively huge, clumsy equipment. Studies of echolocation may help doctors understand better how the brain processes information, and may someday provide similar techniques for blind humans. The female bat's unusual method of sperm storage may aid in livestock fertilization and perhaps improvements in human reproduction. Even the much-maligned vampire bat has made its contribution by helping doctors improve anticoagulation medicines.

One not-so-benign use of bat technology was attempted during World War II, when military scientists devised "Project X-Ray," in which hundreds of bats were to be equipped with miniature incendiary time bombs and parachuted over Osaka, Japan, where it was hoped that they would roost in many of the enemy's wooden buildings and touch them off. The venture proceeded in great secrecy in some of Texas's and New Mexico's bat caves. The first test was successful—in fact, too successful. Six of the bats accidentally torched and destroyed a new air base, whose commander was understandably outraged when told that it was a secret project that could not be divulged even to him. Project X-Ray was abandoned in 1944, evidently because another secret project, the atomic bomb, promised even more devastating firepower.

Despite their immense numbers in some areas, the world bat population is gradually decreasing. Bats have many natural predators. The bat hawk, sometimes called the bat buzzard, of Africa and the East Indies, specializes in bats; one in Zambia was observed catching them at the rate of eighteen per hour. (The bat falcon of South America, despite its name, prefers small birds and insects.) An owl, hawk, peregrine falcon, crow, or even blue jay will catch an occasional bat. A zoologist once watched great horned owls perch at a cave entrance and pick off the bats as they emerged. Many species of snakes feed on bats if other prey is unavailable. Some big brown bats that took refuge in a Maryland attic found it a hazardous haven. It was also occupied by a thirty-eight-inch pilot blacksnake that thrived so well on the bats that it outgrew and shed four skins. Another attic, this one in Salisbury, Vermont, be- came a death trap when someone left a large jar under a leaking roof. One bat fell into it and apparently attracted others with its cries. By the time the jar was noticed again, it held the bodies of 350 bats.

Frogs, fish, opossums, skunks, weasels, squirrels, cats, and other bats will sometimes eat bats. Driver ants can overwhelm a bat colony. And accidents kill many. Bats will sometimes blunder into the huge spiderwebs of the tropics; evidently their echolocation does not easily detect the fine strands of the web. Although bats are skilled at avoiding one another in flight, occasionally the swarm is so crowded that some are forced into barbed wire, tumble onto the hooked barbs of burdock, or become impaled on a cactus plant. Bats have also electrocuted themselves by short-circuiting power lines. Some tree-dwelling bats like to roost in Spanish moss, even though many get caught in it and strangle. Once in a while a bat will meet its end by pouncing on the bait of a mousetrap. Others bog down in tar pits or drown in water holes. Bats can also drown in their roosts when caves flood; one such inundation killed off a quarter of a million in Kentucky's Bat Cave. Hibernating bats can freeze to death during unexpectedly cold weather, as happened to some eight hundred in a Vermont cave during a severe cold spell in 1943. Concentrations of bat guano frequently overheat to the point of spontaneous combustion, asphyxiating the bats in the roost.

But the bat's worst enemy is man, who, on balance, is far more dangerous to the bat than the bat is to man. Insecticides poison insect-eating bats as well as the insects. Pollution kills off many thousands more. In some less civilized parts of the world, the natives hold bat-shooting contests. An International Bat Research Conference held in 1970 agreed that, especially in the temperate zones, bat species were declining, some nearly to extinction. The Jamaican long-tongued bat, the Cuban yellow bat, and the Puerto Rican long-nosed bat are already extinct. In some countries bats are the most threatened species of all mammals.

Bats are legally protected in some of the United States, most European countries, and Mexico. The banning of DDT in the United States has been beneficial to bats as well as birds. But the insecticide has not yet been banned in Mexico, where millions of Mexican free-tails are poisoned by DDT-infected insects during their southern migration. The bats in Carlsbad Caverns have been safeguarded since 1930 by the National Park Service, but not before the caverns' bat population had declined from 8 million to fewer than half a million. Today, Dr. Tuttle warns, nearly 40

percent of all American bat species are officially endangered
or candidates for the Endangered Species List. "Bats," he
says, "are disappearing at a faster rate than any other group
of vertebrates."

Dr. Tuttle's crusade has helped enormously, but chiropterophobia remains a major force. "BCI could make a
lot more money," he says, "if we were trying to get rid of
bats." The rise of environmentalism has not helped the bat
as much as it has more appealing critters. Defenders of old-
growth forests focus on the spotted owl rather than on the
nine bat species that make their homes in dying trees. One
BCI request to an international conservation group for
$25,000 was turned down on the same day that $300,000
was approved for the protection of pandas.

Reading the lore assembled by the bat experts, I could
understand why the Chinese consider the bat a symbol of
good fortune and why some central Asian tribes worship
it. Some American Indians believed that a bat flying into
the house or tepee foretold a good hunting season. Miners
in Nevada are said to be encouraged by the presence of bats
in the tunnels, in this case serving much the same function
as the legendary canary. In Kenya a bat is lucky or unlucky
depending on where it lives. Northern Kenyans believe that
bats promise a good breeding season for their livestock, but
if a bat gets into a house in some parts of western Kenya,
the occupants move out.

Whatever the conflicting attitudes, I can see why the
ugly little beast is certainly worth preserving for its benefit
to all of us, and not least for its fascination. One of the
studies I most liked was done by zoologist Brock Fenton,
who observed the mating scene of hammer-headed bats in
Gabon, Africa. At the beginning of each rainy season the
male bats of the area hang out together on the tree limbs
along the river, flapping their wings, dancing, *kwoking*,

and hooting as the female bats swish past to select their mates, making several passes up and down the line before deciding on a choice. (Fenton calls it a "disco mating strategy," and Tuttle compares the scene to a singles bar.) Fenton recorded that "since the females give a characteristic groan-like call after mating, it is possible to score the number of successes of the males in the assemblage. When the tally is made, it is obvious that the males calling from the middle of the line mate more often than those at the ends." The lucky bats in the middle, Fenton discovered after banding them, occupied the magic location every night, indicating that whatever humans may think of them, at least some bats are not only attractive but irresistible—to other bats. And that, of course, is what counts.

TEN

Swans on the Pond

T H E Y set up housekeeping on an island in a nearby pond, and we spied on them shamelessly with binoculars. By the time I got there, they were building their nest. The cob ("The male—you can tell by the big knob on his bill," one neighbor explained) was scooping weeds from the pond and laying them alongside the nest for the pen (female), who was obviously the interior decorator. She was delicately fashioning the debris into an oval nest about five feet long.

"That will be their home," another swan watcher said. "They'll come back to it every year."

"They mate for life, you know."

"Yes. As Nora Ephron said in her novel, 'If monogamy is what you want, marry a swan.' "

They were large birds, almost four feet tall with their long necks extended. I wondered how old they were. "Five years old, if it's their first nest," another amateur expert explained. "They don't mate until five." Encouraged by his audience, he went on. "But you never can tell the age of a swan. They're just as strong and white at thirty as at five; some of them live to be forty years old."

Big but graceful even as they worked at nest-building,

the swans went methodically about their business until the pen stepped into the center of the nest, shook her feathers, and settled down. "Now she'll lay her eggs," the swan expert predicted. The cob ceased his weed-scooping and strutted around his mate, on guard against any intruders on their new domain.

A handsome couple. I recalled reading about a poll conducted by Yale University and the U.S. Department of the Interior, which found that swans were the third most popular animals in the United States, following dogs and horses and outranking cats, squirrels, robins, and butterflies. Yet even though the swan is America's favorite bird, this tall, white sentinel might be facing a more formidable enemy than he knows, if our state's Department of Environmental Protection has its way.

The mute swan (so called only because it makes less noise than its cousins the tundra and trumpeter swans) came to the United States from England more than a century ago, imported by wealthy Americans to decorate the ponds and lakes on their private estates. These elegant immigrants multiplied and thrived in the New World, especially in the parkland ponds and lagoons of the Eastern suburbs. Sheltered and regularly fed by their human admirers, they have spread down the East Coast and as far west as Michigan and Illinois. Connecticut's mute swan population, for example, has exploded in fewer than two decades from about five hundred to nearly two thousand.

In the process, so the officials at Connecticut's Department of Environmental Protection claim, the swans have driven away other waterfowl by gobbling up more than their share of the aquatic vegetation in the area. So the DEP has advocated a program of swan abortion, proposing that operatives sneak up on the swans' nests and addle the eggs, shaking them to kill the embryos inside. Simply removing the eggs would evidently not work because the swans would produce another fertile clutch.

Egg-addling promptly became a battle cry for swan-lovers and newspaper editorialists in the state. I followed the newspaper reports of this battle with interest, not to say amusement. It was difficult to sympathize with the agents at the DEP, who were given to such bureaucratese statements as "Further population growth [of swans] is not in the best interest of the waterfowl resource"—presumably meaning ducks—"Swans can negatively impact aquatic vegetation in small ponds."

Moreover, the DEP had earlier engaged in a ludicrous campaign against grass carp, a fish many suburbanites imported to stock their ponds, because of the carp's taste for weeds that tend to choke the ponds. Concerned that a few of these Asian fish might escape into the public waterways, eat all the grass, and starve the fish—a dire prediction not confirmed in the ponds, where other fish flourished—the DEP went to the extent of demanding that all the state's carp-inhabited ponds be drained, thereby of course killing not only the carp but all the other fish. Local courts predictably ruled, in effect, that the cure was more draconian than the threat, thereby saving the carp and damaging the credibility of the DEP's carp cops.

The swan-lovers lost no time in charging the DEP with a similar lack of proportion in its campaign against its new villain. Leaders in the battle were some 100,000 members of an organization called Friends of the Animals. Its president, aptly named Priscilla Feral, countered the DEP's claim that Connecticut's swans were endangering other waterfowl by citing the department's own figures: While the state's swan population had grown 56 percent between 1981 and 1986, other waterfowl population had increased 83 percent. (Canada geese had multiplied by more than 100 percent, but that's another chapter.)

"The DEP has the picture of a swan as some sort of aquatic Rambo," Feral complained. Swans, their many supporters argued, far from inhibiting the population of other waterfowl, aided it. With their long necks, the swans reach grass and weeds deeper in the water than smaller birds can, providing leftovers on which they feed.

The National Audubon Society's authoritative *Waterfowl Guide*, the swan fanciers pointed out, states that "swans generally do not compete seriously with ducks but instead often make food available to them by loosening it from the bottom. It is in fact a common sight to see a flock of [ducks] in attendance on a group of feeding swans." The *Waterfowl Guide* adds that swans actually encourage a richer growth of aquatic vegetation for all birds by digging up and cleaning weed-clogged river and lake bottoms. Why, then, the Friends of the Animals acidly inquired, was the Department of Environmental Protection picking on the swan instead of devoting its resources to more important and annoying threats, such as pollution, not to mention the proliferating Canada geese?

The DEP found some supporters, however. Many hunters rose to the defense of other waterfowl, bemoaning the possibility of fewer ducks to kill. There were sinister charges that the "foreign" swans were threatening our noble native American species, a slander that moved Connecticut ornithologist Roger Tory Peterson to observe wryly that "most of us are imports, too."

The DEP also claimed that swans were even dangerous to humans, belligerently attacking people who intruded on their nesting sites, though the DEP did not explain why any critter should be expected *not* to defend its nesting territory (especially if the intruder intends to addle its eggs).

Meanwhile, a former neighbor of mine who had moved to Mississippi was writing me about a different swan problem in his town. His neighbors, anxious to replace some swans that had died, had found a local supplier who was asking four hundred dollars or more per bird. I was tempted to enter the Connecticut controversy with the suggestion that some of our swans be shipped to Mississippi. But I decided against it for fear of inciting an even more controversial rash of swan-napping.

Some of the state's other ornithologists did agree with the DEP, arguing that fewer swans are better than too many swans, even for the swans' own good. Finally a state legislator came to the swans' rescue by citing the Fourth Amendment of the Constitution. Egg-addlers, he pointed out, would have to enter private property where swans were nesting. "The Fourth Amendment," he reminded his fellow legislators, "says you're secure in your home and free from search and seizure." Whether or not the legislators felt they were applying the amendment to swans as well as citizens, the Legislative Regulation Review Committee of the General Assembly blocked the DEP's project. As of this writing, the swan protectors have continued to hold the egg-addlers at bay.

Studying our swans, I opted to be an anti–egg addler. I have been an amateur swan-watcher for many years, and in my neighborhood, at least, there have never been too many of them. Sometimes a dozen have paraded grandly across the pond or cove in our neighborhood in a line like a great white fleet, their heads cocked high on their slender, curving necks, their large but streamlined bodies moving effortlessly through the water. But I realized that my area was what ornithologists would call a small habitat sample for observation. So I went off to the local library, came home staggering under a pile of bird books, and settled down for a more thorough study of the swan, supplemented by conversations with a few experts on the genus *Cygnus*.

The mute swan *(Cygnus olor)* is one of nearly a dozen species of swan that inhabit every continent except Africa and Antarctica (though some visit the latter on occasion). Some swan bones have been dated to the time of the disappearance of the dinosaurs. In fact, swans may have been the first waterfowl. American swans come in three different species, the mute in the East, the tundra swan—formerly called the whistling swan—*(Cygnus columbianus)* ranging all across North America, and the trumpeter *(Cygnus buccinator)* from the Atlantic seaboard to the Midwest.

Most of the swans in my area stay here throughout the year; if the ponds freeze, they fly to the open salt water of the nearby coves and harbors. But their western cousins the tundra swans perform marvels of migration from their summer nests near the Arctic Ocean to the warmer waters of the Southern states. They are generally the last to take off from the icy lakes and ponds, knowing that with their speed they will catch up with the ducks and geese that have preceded them.

A veteran cob takes the point of their V formation, and the herd (ornithologists call a flock of swans a herd) climbs rapidly to a mile or more of altitude. The swans head straight south overland, rarely dropping down to feed or rest en route. Their flying wedge provides a slipstream to pull along each bird behind the point. "Swans, unlike soaring birds, have to propel themselves through the air," says the Connecticut Audubon Society's ornithologist, Milan Bull. "And because they are large, heavy birds, they very quickly learn the path of least resistance." Occasionally the leader will drop back and let another strong cob take the point, resuming the lead position as soon as he has rested. British ornithologist Lillian Paca claims that the still-dusky cygnets of the herd fly slightly above their parents so that when they tire they can drop onto their parents' backs for a free ride. Yale University's Charles Sibley doubts this, pointing out that "an airborne swan is heavy enough without the extra weight of a young passenger."

I have never forgotten the first time I heard the high-flying tundras (they were still called whistlers then)—the bass horn of the elders punctuated by the flute trills of the cygnets—one year when we were living in Illinois. As Roger Tory Peterson points out, these big birds often can be "heard long before [they] can be detected in the sky." I remember that it took me some time to spot them. With their thirty-pound bodies stretched out in flight, their necks extended straight out, and their legs tucked under their tails, the herd resembled a huge white arrowhead in the sky. The tundra swan's powerful six-foot wingspread propels it along at up to fifty miles an hour; with a strong tailwind, some have been clocked at nearly one hundred miles an hour. (One speeding tundra collided with a plane at six thousand feet and forced it into a crash landing.) When they encounter storms they climb even higher; ice crystals form on their wings, but they fly on over mountains and plains to their southern destination, finally swooping down to splash into a lake or bay, gabbling at each other in relief and gobbling up everything edible.

Tundra swans tend to keep away from human habitation; a notable exception was a renegade tundra that, about thirty years ago, took a perverse delight in spooking the cows on an Oregon dairy farm, chasing them every time they approached their feeding troughs. When some of the stampeding cattle were injured, the farmer caught the swan and shipped it to a zoo, where it had to settle for chasing ducks.

The larger trumpeter is less wary of civilization, and as a result nearly became extinct. The largest American swan—in fact the biggest of all waterfowl—measuring five and a half feet from bill to tail and weighing up to forty pounds, with an impressive ten-foot wingspan, the trumpeter is so named because its longer windpipe emits a deep bassoon call, especially sonorous during the mating season. In the early nineteenth century the trumpeter was a familiar sight in Oregon, Washington, and northern California, and migrated over the Midwest to the Atlantic coast. But because of its unwariness the trumpeter was easily slaughtered for its warm swansdown. (John James Audubon wrote that trumpeter feather quills were "so hard, and yet so elastic" that they were better than steel pens for his drawings.) By 1918 a federal Migratory Bird Treaty Act banned the sale of bird skins and feathers, but it was almost too late to save the trumpeter, whose population had plummeted; by 1933, fewer than one hundred were left in the entire United States.

The trumpeter's savior was the Red Rocks Lake National Wildlife Refuge, established in 1935 in the Centennial Valley of southwestern Montana. Today this refuge harbors so many trumpeter swans that newborn cygnets are moved to nearby wildlife parks—partly because the trumpeters at Red Rocks Lake do not bother to migrate. The valley's lakes and ponds are warmed by the same underground heat that produces Yellowstone Park's geysers. So the swans (also nourished by about one thousand bushels of grain ladled out by the U.S. Fish and Wildlife Service each winter) are content to stay put. At the latest count, the U.S. trumpeter population had risen to fifteen thousand.

In the mid-1920s a couple dozen trumpeters found refuge on British Columbia's Lonesome Lake, adjoining the farm of one Ralph Edwards, whose thirteen-year-old daughter, Trudy, fed them with grain. Over the years the news spread by word of beak, and the Edwards farm became a gathering place for trumpeters, some of them tame enough to eat from Trudy's hand. The Canadian government officially designated Edwards and his daughter "swan wardens" and supplied the grain. But then someone had the bright idea of making a gift of a few trumpeters to England's Princess Elizabeth, and Trudy was asked to capture them. She lured five trumpeters into a trap and they were flown to England. Not another trumpeter came near Trudy Edwards for four years. (The captured trumpeters meanwhile thrived in a British swan sanctuary.)

Ornithologists today are attempting to foster a trumpeter renascence in Michigan with the unwitting help of the mute swans flourishing in the area. Recently some scientists transported a few trumpeter eggs—packed in Styrofoam and warmed by hot-water bottles—from a Kansas City zoo to Kalamazoo, Michigan, where they were surreptitiously deposited in a mute swan's nest, in the hope that the involuntary foster parents would not notice when some of their eggs hatched into gray instead of beige cygnets, with black instead of orange bills. At last report the mute swans had not rejected the intruders.

Other countries have other swans. The European whooper is so similar to the American trumpeter that it was once thought to be the same species. The Russian Jankowski swan migrates all the way to China and Japan. On the island of Rugen, in the Baltic Sea, peasants once believed that the local immutable swan brought babies by special delivery; it can fly three times as fast as the stork. That continent of unique animals, Australia, has a black swan; herds of them come out to escort ocean liners into the harbor at Perth, whose Swan River is named after them.

South America has a white swan with a black neck. Argentina has a swan-goose. And England has the dainty Bewick's swan, so small that it is sometimes mistaken for a snow goose.

But England's best-known swan is the ancestor of the mutes my neighbors and I were watching. Although there is a legend that the swan was introduced to England by Julius Caesar, the species long antedated the Romans. The mute swan has been England's royal bird ever since King Canute set the precedent in 1023 of awarding "Games and Flights of Swannes" to a courtier "for his amiable fidelity."

It was Elizabeth I who proclaimed that all swans not privately owned belonged to the crown, promptly overcrowding her swannery.

Semidomesticated as early as the twelfth century, the British mute swan has long since learned to coexist comfortably with humans. Because they are protected by the crown, swans swarm over England's rivers, ponds, and estuaries. And unlike Connecticut's DEP and duck hunters, the British enjoy them. On a recent visit to Henley, we had to pick our way through them as they sunned themselves on the riverbank, and at every pub along the Thames the diners are expected to share their lunch with swans that nearly outnumber—and arrogantly outmaneuver—the ducks and geese.

A memorable twentieth-century example was a cob named Godfrey whose habitat was a quarry on the Isle of Man until a storm bashed him against the rocks and broke his wing. He was rescued and taken to a lake on Sir Douglas Young's estate near Castletown, where Godfrey soon became homesick and set out for his quarry home. Unable to fly because of his injured wing, he waddled down the main road. But a swan's feet hurt if it walks too far; so when Godfrey reached town, he paused to rest at the railroad station. The stationmaster recognized Godfrey and telephoned Lady Young to report, "M'lady, your swan's standing in the ticket queue, waiting to buy a ticket. What shall I do?" Lady Young drove into town, scooped up Godfrey, and took him to his quarry. He swam about until his nostalgia evidently was satisfied, then hopped back into the car to return to the Young estate.

The swans of Wells, England, have even learned to call for their dinner. In the moat of an ancient palace there is a string attached to a bell; the swans pull the string to ring the bell when hungry, and bread is tossed to them. Like the ducks in the United States that follow the swans, the Wells ducks, not large enough to reach the string, subsist on the swans' crumbs.

The British Isles seem to have nearly as many eccentric swans as humans. Most of those in London, for some reason best known to themselves, refuse to swim under the Thames bridges, preferring to fly over them, even though they often collide with the double-decker buses. And another Isle of Man swan, named Johnny, was a tourist attraction in the harbor town of Peel. Johnny, decked out in a ribbon with a bell around his neck, met the summer visitors and led them on a waddling tour of the town, inevitably ending at a fish store, where he patiently awaited a kipper tip.

The mute swan is nearly as domesticated in the United States. The pair we were spying on not only did not mind the intrusion but frequently swam over to the shore for handouts. (Another hungry neighborhood swan meanwhile ventured as far as a local restaurant half a mile from the nearest water, became disoriented, and had to be rescued.) The bird books had cautioned me not to feed them bread; eel grass and other greens are better for them. But our swans obviously had not read the same books; they gobbled up my neighbors' breadcrumbs more eagerly than the greenery I offered them. Ornithologist Bull explains that swans also need carbohydrates for body fat, "and since human habitation has taken away many of the fields they might forage in, they are quite willing to settle for grains converted into bread." Yale's Sibley adds, "It's the swan's version of junk food—white bread tastes great." But since a swan eats up to twelve pounds of food a day, a few pieces of junk food probably do not distort its dietary requirements.

It turned out that I had missed our swans' mating; and

when I read about it I was sorry not to have seen it. Their elaborate courtship display starts with the cob chasing the pen about the pond. If another cob or even a goose or duck gets too close, he goes into what ornithologists call his "busking act" or "threat display." Raising his wings, lowering his neck along his back, hissing, snorting, and flapping, he chases the intruder away. When he returns to his mate, she joins him in the "triumph ceremony." Arching their wings, they swim toward each other until they touch; they rub cheeks, waggle their bills, shake their feathers, and snort in victorious unison.

By now the pen is ready too. Together they pirouette in the water, necks extended, bills bobbing. Facing each other and synchronizing their movements, they preen their feathers and dip their bills, and sometimes even their necks and heads, in the water. Shortly the pen subsides in the water with her neck stretched straight out. And as they mate she exhales a long, sighing call. Then they face each other again, rise in the water, touch breasts and cheeks, emit a final snort, and settle back amid much feather-shaking. Age does not seem to dim the swan's ardor; forty-year-old pairs that have produced some two hundred offspring have continued to put on the same vigorous, affectionate display year after year.

Soon they are at work building their nest—which was where I came in with our two. Gradually their nest rose two or three feet, a huge, ungainly looking collection of sticks, weeds, and detritus that was actually a marvel of construction: soft, springy, porous, yet (according to some bird books) buoyant enough to float if the area was flooded. In this new nursery, as March turned into April, the pen deposited half a dozen eggs, and both expectant parents settled down for about five weeks of incubation.

Usually the pen is the incubator and the cob the protec-

tor of the nest. But occasionally our cob briefly spelled the
pen over the eggs. Changing the guard, we saw, was nearly
as ceremonious as the courtship. The returning pen waddled to the nest and stroked the cob's bill with hers. They
twined their necks and rubbed their bills through each
other's feathers. The cob rose from the nest and gently
turned the eggs over with his feet. He and the pen stood
together admiring their eggs. Then the cob stepped aside,
the pen climbed into the nest, carefully settled down, shook
herself, laid her neck along her back, and buried her head
in her feathers.

Often both parents left the eggs uncovered, though
camouflaged with a few twigs from the nest. "The eggs
need occasional cooling," ornithologist Bull explains.
"Sometimes the pen will even sprinkle them with water.
It's like a shot in the arm for the embryos inside the eggs,
to keep them stimulated and healthy."

The protective cob has many predators to contend
with, including raccoons, foxes, weasels, large gulls, turtles, and water rats, not to mention egg-addlers from the
DEP. But a cob guarding his nest is a formidable foe; the
force of his powerful wing, which has a hard knob at its
leading edge, can kill a small animal. There is one account
of a Canadian trumpeter swan driving a bull moose into
ignominious retreat. No doubt the mute swan's defense of
its nest has helped give it a reputation for belligerence.
And an occasional ornery, hungry swan will be aggressive
enough to go on the attack. But when they are not defending their nests, most swans are mild-mannered. In fact,
I once watched a pair of swimming mutes driven away from
the shore by the dive-bombing and head-pecking of a tiny,
angry red-winged blackbird defending its turf.

Swans, too, are territorial, and they need a lot of territory; one pair can dominate an entire pond. But the parents

we were watching, far from being belligerent, took their turns swimming over to us for food.

The bird books report that if the cob is on the nest when the eggs begin to hatch, he beats a quick retreat and lets the pen take over the maternal duties, gently sitting on the wet little cygnets until they are dry and fluffy, and tossing the eggshells out of the nest. Our newborn swans, diminutive blobs of beige fluff alongside their big parents, were quickly able to totter about the nest. There were four of them; two of the eggs had not hatched. "This is the most dangerous time," says Bull. "Cold, wet spring weather can kill many newborn cygnets." But ours survived. Within a few days they were waddling down to the water's edge, where the cob was on duty, teaching them how to paddle about. The pen remained in the nest until the last cygnet was in the water.

Shortly the entire family was sailing across the pond in single file, the pen in the lead and the cob bringing up the rear, on the lookout for snapping turtles, which have a nasty habit of grabbing cygnets by the feet and pulling them under. When an errant youngster strayed out of line, the cob quickly herded it back, scolding it for its transgression. When a cygnet occasionally tired of swimming, it climbed onto a parent's back until it had rested; if one fell off, it received another scolding.

For the first week or so the parents pulled up weeds for their youngsters; but after about ten days they were nudging the cygnets under the tail, teaching them to upend for their food. Usually after an hour or two of swimming and feeding, the family returned to its nest. I have noticed that most of the songbirds in our neighborhood desert their nests as soon as the fledglings have learned to fly. Not so these swans, which used their nest as home base throughout the summer. By autumn, when the cygnets are able to get along on their own, the parents usually remain in their empty nest; if they leave it for the winter, they return in the spring to raise the next brood. Some pairs of swans use the same nest to raise twenty to thirty broods of young. Most of the bird books claim that swans mate for life, but zoologists have recently discovered that swans, like many other birds and animals, can frequently commit adultery.

So domesticated was our swan family that the parents were soon leading their cygnets to the shoreline for the food I offered, teaching the youngsters to fend for themselves by competing with them for whatever I tossed into the water. While they fed, I noticed that mute swans were far from mute; they muttered, chuckled, and snorted. A mute swan can also hiss, growl, trill, bark, and even give a loud cry when alarmed.

The cygnets know by instinct how to preen—to stroke the oil from the glands near the tail to waterproof their feathers. Their acquired education includes nest-building. Some parents select a site and teach the youngsters how to dredge up the material and fashion a nest, abandoning it when the lesson is over. But the most spectacular part of the cygnets' learning process is flying.

A thirty-to-forty-pound mute swan takes off like an overloaded bomber. Its eight-foot wingspan beats heavily as the swan runs along the surface of the water, gradually gaining speed for up to one hundred yards until it finally becomes airborne. Audubon once described the takeoff of a herd of swans on the ice, the pounding of their feet "like the noise of great muffled drums." Long before man and his airplane, the swan learned the aerodynamics of flight, taking off and landing into the wind. After many years I can still recall the sensation as a pair of swans came in for a landing right over my head while I was walking on our beach. I heard their huge, whistling wings make the air throb before I saw them wheel down behind me, thrust their feet out, backwind their wings for drag, and splash into the water, shaking their feathers and waggling their tails as they proceeded grandly out to sea.

Our cygnets were not given flight training until they were nearly half-grown and their wings had developed. Watching their parents' booming takeoffs, the cygnets imitated the maneuver, at first nose-diving and cartwheeling back into the water. Their initial flights were only fifty feet or so, but gradually they learned to climb higher and fly greater distances alongside their parents.

These tawny little birds, still in the fuzz of youth, were already assuming a regal pose, necks arched and bills tucked in as they glided across the pond. Ornithologist Paca claims that mute swans are quite aware of their attractive appearance and even work at it; Milan Bull agrees that "swans do a lot of posturing, but for other swans, not humans." In any case, the swan is one of nature's loveliest creatures. No wonder the ancients linked them with Aphrodite, the goddess of love, and Apollo, the god of poetry. According to myth, when Jupiter had designs on the lovely Leda, he chose the guise of a swan as the most likely to win her favor. (The liaison produced triplets: Castor, Pollux, and a girl whose beauty would cause a war, Helen of Troy.)

The swan has been celebrated even more by artists, poets, and composers than by ornithologists. The Valkyries of Wagnerian opera were swan maidens that carried dead warriors to the Nordic heaven, Valhalla. And of course one of the world's best-loved ballets is *Swan Lake*. A private swan refuge in Abbotsbury, England, is closed to visitors during the mating season—except on an occasion some years ago when Anna Pavlova was permitted to study them while rehearsing for her role as Odette-Odile in *Swan Lake*.

Perhaps the most enduring legend is that of the "swan song," the melodious, haunting cry of a dying swan. The legend was originated by Socrates as he prepared to drink his fatal potion of hemlock. "I do not believe swans sing in sorrow," he told his grieving followers. "I think, because they are prophets, they know the good things in the other world. I depart life no more dispirited than they." The more mundane explanation is that a dying swan may give one last exhalation from its long windpipe. But as Yale's Sibley puts it, "the romantic notion of the dying swan song is pure myth."

One of our swans unfortunately proved this fact—when late in the summer the cob wandered onto the road and was unable to waddle out of the way of an auto coming around the corner. He died quietly and quickly. His bereaved mate stood guard over his body until it was taken away. She remained in the nest and the pond, continuing to school her cygnets until in the autumn they were able to fend for themselves. Then all of them disappeared.

Next spring I watched for her return, but the nest remained unoccupied. What had become of her? Perhaps, with last year's cygnets grown and departed, she had taken another mate. If so, I hoped it was in another state, far from the threat of egg-addlers after her newest brood.

Acknowledgments

R ARELY is a nonfiction book a solo effort. There are usually dozens of experts on the subject, participants to be interviewed and savvy librarians without whom the work could not be assembled.

This book could not have been assembled without the help of a hundred or more collaborators, most of them neighbors who have also had to cope with wildlife in the suburbs. Their encounters make up a sizable portion of the book, and I'm grateful to them all.

Kirk Miles is the neighbor who tossed mothballs down the skunk's hole, only to have them tossed back; Kirk is also the host who provided the macadamia nut for the delighted squirrel. Bob McDonald is the only man I know who has outwitted a raccoon. Dave and Janet Caulkins supplied many anecdotes; and it was their friend Gretchen Petersen who had to deal with a raccoon on fire.

The late Peggy Park, who became familiar with more animals than she cared to because of her cat door, is the neighbor who put the opossum into spin in her clothes dryer; she was also the one who tipped me off that skunks like tuna fish.

Tom Bria is the friend whose family doesn't want him

to shoot a doe. Dave Shields is the neighbor who lost the steak to the gull. Sandy Brown is the breakfaster who found himself face to face with a raccoon in the cereal closet. The late Ned Shippen always claimed that the pair of raccoons he transported into the countryside got back to our suburb the same day he did. Al Munkenbeck was the one who discovered that Big Macs make perfect raccoon bait.

Ray Haney, who runs around Greenwich Point every day, encounters some critter on every run. It was Mary Ellen LeBien who told me about the bats in a local church. Dr. Paul Yudkofsky, who, like me, believes in the principle of live-and-let-live, has more raccoon stories than even I could use.

I also had help from a veritable network of friends far and wide. Bob Donnelly, who moved from our suburb to one in Mississippi, has kept me up to date on the swan situation there. Adrienne Gunst has likewise sent periodical bulletins on the deer situation in the San Francisco suburbs. It was my college roommate Dave Martin, in a suburb of Philadelphia, who invented that squirrel-shocking bird feeder. Dave, like so many of my friends, has gone to the Great Suburb in the Sky; but if there are any pesky critters there, he knows how to deal with them.

Dick and Sally Wheeler have not let a critter go unreported in their Boston area; I'm indebted to them for regular bulletins. Van Messner of Wilton, Connecticut, was the first to alert me to the return of the coyote to our area. It was Phil Wootton who spotted the well-fed coyote on his lawn in New Canaan. Ames Richards is the friend who turned to verse to lament the odious presence of Canada geese on his pondside lawn in Stamford. I'm grateful to Anne Geismar of Harrison, New York, for her deer-repellant recipe. That legendary *Life* photographer, Loomis Dean, keeps me apprised on the squirrel (and alligator) situation in Florida. George and Barbara Brownell keep me up to date on the raccoons in Vermont. It was while visiting Trudy Harris's ranch in the Texas hill country that I heard those serenading Texas-size mockingbirds.

My friend Gouverneur "Nick" Nichols pointed out to me that there are more deer in his suburban New Canaan, Connecticut, backyard than on his Vermont farm. Dan Wolk, in his delightful book on suburban living, *The Dirt from Tripp Street*, is the friend who slyly suggested that Westchester nurserymen might be encouraging the deer. Don Weadon of Weston, Connecticut, is the friend who missed the raccoon and shot his Buick. Jane Scholl in Washington, D.C., passed along the tip that a shampoo got the skunk smell off our mutual friend Nancy Shuker's dog Dudley. And it was the late Walter Pettit of South Salem, New York, who first suggested to me that the bat has had a bum rap.

Even friends abroad have been helpful. Russell and Renate Miller swapped houses with us one recent August, enabling me to do some amateur field research on the British rabbit. While there, I was able to check out with our English friends David and Rosamund Raymond the time when, about to rent our house, David and I confronted the skunk in the cellar.

I owe a big vote of thanks to the zoologists and ornithologists who were so helpful, particularly Milan Bull of the Connecticut Audubon Society; Stephen Keller of Yale, who ran the poll that found the swan America's most popular bird; and Charles Sibley, who has to rescue Canada geese beaned by balls on the Yale Golf Course. Not to mention Merlin Tuttle, who can keep you spellbound for hours with his stories about bats.

Unlike many writers, I have had excellent editors. My former boss at *Life* magazine, E. K. Thompson, founded

Smithsonian magazine, in which he published my battle report on raccoons in my garbage. His son, E. T. Thompson, editor-in-chief of *Reader's Digest*, encouraged me to write more such accounts; and with the shrewd editing of Tom Lashnits and other *Digest* editors, I told their millions of readers about some of my encounters with gulls, squirrels, and that skunk in the cellar. The readers responded in great numbers; I now have more designs for squirrel-proof bird feeders, for example, than I can test in my lifetime. I thank all those, too many to list, who sent me *their* stories of dealing with critters in the suburbs.

Literary agent Julian Bach had the imagination to see the possibility of a book in these encounters, as did Tom Dunne, who not only agreed to publish the book under his imprint, but also provided the discerning, patient editing it needed. My thanks also to Associate Editor Pete Wolverton and especially to David Smith for excellent copyediting.

My long-suffering family tolerated years of critter-watching with books and binoculars for what must have seemed to them a silly project after the heavy volumes of maritime history I had previously produced. My wife, Jane, who worked with me on all of my books, helped with this one too, but did not live to see it in print. Our son Chris, with his friend Duncan Highman, got that skunk out of our cellar, and then opted for life in the city instead of the suburbs. Our daughter Ann Marr, who lives in Westchester County, has provided countless examples of adaptive wildlife, and her daughters Abby and Melissa have added more.

But it's the critters themselves—sometimes friendly and funny, sometimes wary and wise—who were essential to this book. They are its heroes, as they should be.

Bibliography

Most of my research, if that is the word, was done in the habitat of Old Greenwich, Connecticut, which I share with the many critters I've described. Newspapers have recounted incidents similar to my own encounters, especially *The New York Times*, *Greenwich Time*, *Greenwich News*, *The Boston Globe*, *The San Francisco Chronicle* and the Nantucket *Inquirer and Mirror*. So have such magazines as *Reader's Digest*, *Smithsonian*, *Time*, *Newsweek*, *Scientific American*, *Modern Maturity*, *Bats*, *The Bird Watcher's Digest* and many scientific publications. The following books were particularly helpful.

GENERAL

Anthony, H. E., Ed. *Animals of America*. Garden City, New York: Garden City Publishing Co., 1937.

Bellrose, Frank C. *Ducks, Geese and Swans of North America*. New York: Stackpole, 1942.

Birds of Sea, Shore and Stream. New York: *Wild, Wild World of Animals* Series, Time-Life Films, 1976.

Carrington, Richard. *The Mammals*. New York: *Life Nature Library*, Time-Life Books, 1963.

Collins, Henry Hill, Jr., Ed. *Bent's Life Histories of American Birds*. New York: Harper & Brothers, 1960.

Dorst, Jean. *The Life of Birds*. New York: Columbia University Press, 1974.

Forbush, Edward Howe, Revised by John Richard May. *Natural History of the Birds of Eastern and Central North America*. Boston: Houghton-Mifflin, 1939.

Godin, Alfred J. *Wild Mammals of New England*. Baltimore, MD: Johns Hopkins University Press, 1977.

Gruson, Edward S. *Words for Birds: A Lexicon for North American Birds with Biographical Notes.* New York: New York Times Co., 1972.

Hausman, Leon Augustus. *The Illustrated Encyclopedia of American Birds.* New York: Halcyon House, 1944.

Johnsgard, Paul A. *A Guide to North American Waterfowl.* Bloomington, Indiana: Indiana University Press, 1979.

Jordan, William. *Divorce Among the Gulls: An Uncommon Look at Human Nature.* San Francisco: North Point Press, 1991.

Lincoln, Frederick C. *The Migration of American Birds.* New York: Doubleday, Dowan, 1939.

Matthews, L. Harrison. *The Life of Mammals.* New York: Universe Books, 1970.

Palmer, Ralph S., Ed. *Handbook of North American Birds.* New Haven: Yale University Press, 1976.

Pearson, T. Gilbert, Ed. *Birds of America.* New York: University Society, Inc., 1923.

Peterson, Roger Tory. *A Field Guide to the Birds: Eastern Land and Water Birds.* Boston: Houghton-Mifflin, 1934.

Pough, Richard H. *Audubon Water Bird Guide.* New York: Doubleday, 1951.

Sanders, Scott Russell, Ed. *Audubon Reader: The Best Writings of John James Audubon.* Bloomington, IN: Indiana University Press, 1986.

Seton, Ernest Thompson. *Life Histories of Northern Animals.* New York: Scribner's, 1909.

———. *Lives of Game Animals.* Boston: Charles T. Branford, 1953.

Wetmore, Alexander. *Song and Garden Birds of North America.* Washington, D.C.: National Geographic Society; 1964.

———. *Water, Prey and Game Birds of North America.* Washington, D.C.: National Science Library, 1965.

SKUNKS

Blassingame, Wyatt. *Skunks.* New York: Dodd, Mead, 1981.

Cott, Hugh Branford. *Adaptive Coloration in Animals.* London: Oxford University Press, 1940.

Hess, Lilo. *The Misunderstood Skunk.* New York: Scribner's, 1969.

Hume, Charles. *Skunks as Pets.* Fond du Lac, WI: All-Pets Books, 1957.

Patent, Dorothy Hinshaw. *Weasels, Otters, Skunks and Their Family.* New York: Holiday House, 1973.

Zistel, Era. *Thistle & Co.* Boston: Little, Brown, 1981.

RACCOONS

Gilbert, Bil. "Who Can Resist a Raccoon?" *Reader's Digest*, May 1979.

Holmgren, Virginia C. *Raccoons*. Santa Barbara, CA: Capra Press, 1990.

Leslie, Robert Frank. *Ringo, the Robber Raccoon*. New York: Dodd, Mead, 1984.

MacClintock, Douglas. *A Natural History of Raccoons*. New York: Scribner's, 1981.

North, Sterling. *Raccoons are the Brightest People*. New York: Dutton, 1965.

Redford, Polly. *Raccoons and Eagles: Two Views of American Wildlife*. New York: Dutton, 1965.

Rue, Leonard Lee III. *The World of the Raccoon*. Philadelphia: Lippincott, 1964.

Schinner, James R., and Darrell L. Cauley. *The Ecology of Urban Raccoons in Cincinnati, Ohio*. Cincinnati, OH: University of Cincinnati Press, 1974.

SQUIRRELS

Adler, Bill, Jr. *Outwitting Squirrels*. Chicago: Chicago Review Press, 1988.

Barkalow, Frederick S., and Monica Shorten. *The World of the Gray Squirrel*. Philadelphia: Lippincott, 1973.

Batcheller, G., and B. Tullar. "A New Look at an Old Friend." *Conservationist*, Sept.–Oct. 1984.

Davies, Adrian. *Discovering Squirrels*. New York: The Bookwright Press, 1987.

DeCoursey, P. J. "Daily Light-Sensitivity Rhythm in a Rodent." *Science*, Jan. 1, 1960.

Farmer, C. J. "Summertime Squirrels." *Outdoor Life*, Apr. 1986.

Gilbert, Bil. "When Squirrels Go Nuts." *Audubon*, July 1980.

Graham, Ada and Frank. *We Watch Squirrels*. New York: Dodd, Mead, 1985.

Gurnell, John. *The Natural History of Squirrels*. Washington, D.C.: Facts on File, 1987.

Kinkead, Eugene. *The Squirrel Book*. New York: Dutton, 1980.

———. "Those White House Squirrels." *Audubon*, Sept. 1984.

Mills, E. M. "Control of Tree Squirrels." *Consumer Bulletin*, Sept. 1965.

North, Sterling. *Rascal*. New York: Dutton, 1963.

Ryden, Hope. "A Red Squirrel's Life is More than Just a Tempest in a Treetop." *Smithsonian*, Nov. 1991.

Spruch, Grace Marmor. *Such Agreeable Friends*. New York: Morrow, 1983.

Stokes, Donald and Lillian. *The Bird Feeder Book*. Boston: Little, Brown, 1987.
Zistel, Era. "Gentlest Pets I ever Had." *Saturday Evening Post*, Dec. 27, 1958.

CANADA GEESE

Bevier, Louis R. *Management of the Canada Goose (Branta Canadensis) in the Town of Greenwich*. Greenwich, CT: Greenwich Conservation Commission, 1992.
Gorman, James. "Taking a Gander at the Geese of Greenwich." *Discover*, Nov. 1983.
Owen, Myrfen. *Wild Geese of the World*. London: B.T. Botsford, 1980.
Sweet, Ozzie and Jack Denton Scott. *Canada Geese*. New York: Putnam's, 1976.
Van Wormer, Joe. *The World of the Canada Goose*. Philadelphia: Lippincott, 1968.

DEER

Adams, Anne B. and Nancy Nash Cummings. *Dear Anne and Nan*. New York: Bantam, 1992.
Gilbert, Bil. "Coyotes Have Adapted to Us, Now We Have to Adapt to Them." *Smithsonian*, Mar. 1991.
Heuser, Ken. "What's Happening to Our Deer?" *Field & Stream*, Oct. 1971.
Jescavage-Bernard, Karen. *Gardening in Deer Country*. Croton on Hudson, New York: Privately printed by K. J.B., 1992.
Laycock, George. *Whitetail: The Story of a White-Tailed Deer*. New York: Norton, 1966.
Madson, John. *The White-Tailed Deer*. East Alton, IL: Olin Mathieson Chemical Corp., 1961.
Mason, George F. *The Deer Family*. New York: Morrow, 1962.
Matschke, George H. "Micro-incapsulated Diethylstielrol as an Oral Contraceptive in White-Tailed Deer." *Journal of Wildlife Management*, 41, no. 1 (1987).
Newsom, William Manypenny. *Whitetailed Deer*. New York: Scribner's, 1926.
Ozaga, John J. "Response of Whitetailed Deer to Winter Weather." *Journal of Wildlife Management*, July 1969.
Pruitt, William O., Jr. "Rutting Behavior of the Whitetail Deer." *Journal of Mammology*, 35, no. 1 (1954).
Rue, Leonard Lee III. *The Deer of North America*. Danbury, CT: Outdoor Life Books, 1989.

————. *The World of the White-Tailed Deer*. Philadelphia: Lippincott, 1962.

Severinghaus, C. W. and Benjamin F. Tuller, Jr. "Wintering Deer Versus Snowmobiles." *The Conservationist*, June–July 1975.

Statfeld, Curtis K. *Whitetail Deer: A Year's Cycle*. New York: Dial Press, 1975.

Sweeney, J. R. R., Larry Marchinton and J.M. Sweeney. "Responses of Radio-Monitored White-Tailed Deer Chased by Dogs." *Journal of Wildlife Management*, 35, no. 4 (1971).

Taylor, W. P., Ed. *The Deer of North America*. Washington, D.C.: Stackpole, 1956.

Verme, Louis J., and John J. Ozoga. "Sex Ratio of White-Tailed Deer and the Estrus Cycle." *Journal of Wildlife Management*, 45, no. 3 (1981).

Warner, Roger. "Ticks and Deer Team Up to Cause Trouble for Man." *Smithsonian*, Apr. 1986.

Whitehead, G. Kenneth. *Deer of the World*. New York: Viking, 1972.

GULLS

Bent, Arthur Cleveland. *Life Histories of North American Gulls and Terns*. Washington, D.C.: Smithsonian Institution, Bulletin 113, Government Printing Office, 1921.

Costello, David F. *The World of the Gull*. Philadelphia: Lippincott, 1971.

Darling, Louis. *The Gull's Way*. New York: Morrow, 1965.

Edey, Maitland. *The Northeast Coast*. New York: Time-Life Books, 1972.

Graham, Frank, Jr. *Gulls: A Social History*. New York: Random House, 1975.

Hopson, Janet. "Gulls Have a Lot of Gall." *National Wildlife*, Feb.–Mar. 1982.

Howell, Thomas R. "Desert-Nesting Sea Gulls." *Natural History*, Aug. 1982.

Hunt, George and Molly. "Female-Female Pairing in Western Gulls *(Larus occidentalis)* in Southern California." *Science*, June 24, 1979.

Jackson, Donald Dale. "The Bad and the Beautiful: Gulls Remind Us of Us." *Smithsonian*, Oct. 1989.

Kirkpatrick, Sean J. "Gulls: A Sea Guide." *Sea Frontiers*, May–June 1989.

Miller, David S., David Peakall, and William B. Kintner. "Ingestion of Crude Oil: Sublethal Effects in Herring Gull Chicks." *Science*, Jan. 20, 1978.

Nash, Ogden. *Verses from 1929 On*. Boston: Little, Brown, 1940.

Schmidt-Nielsen, Knut. "Salt Glands." *Scientific American*, Jan. 1959.

Smith, Neal Griffith. "Visual Isolation in Gulls." *Scientific American*, Oct. 1967.

Storer, John H. "Bird Aerodynamics." *Scientific American*, Apr. 1952.

Tinbergen, Nikolaas. "The Evolution of Behavior in Gulls." *Scientific American*, Dec. 1960.

———. *The Herring Gull's World*. London: 1953.

Tucker, Vance A. "The Energetics of Bird Flight." *Scientific American*, May 1969.

Welty, Carl. "Birds As Flying Machines." *Scientific American*, March 1955.

MOCKINGBIRDS

Doughty, Robin W. *The Mockingbird*. Austin, Texas: University of Texas Press, 1988.

Gurin, Joel. "There's More to Bird Songs Than the Sound of Music." *Smithsonian*, July 1982.

Harrison, Kit & George. *America's Favorite Backyard Birds*. New York: Simon & Schuster, 1983.

Kastner, Joseph. *The Bird Illustrated: 1500–1900*. From the Collection of the New York Public Library. New York: Harry Abrams, 1988.

Lee, Harper. *To Kill a Mockingbird*. Philadelphia: Lippincott, 1960.

Lembke, Janet. *Dangerous Birds: A Naturalist's Aviary*. New York: Lyons & Burford, 1992.

Matthews, F. Schuyler. *Field Book of Wild Birds and Their Music*. New York: Putnam, 1940.

McCullough, David. *Truman*. New York: Simon & Schuster, 1992.

Ogburn, Charlton. *The Adventure of Birds*. New York: Morrow, 1976.

RABBITS

Hanzak, John, Zdenek Veselovsky, and David Stephen. *Collins Encyclopedia of Animals*. London: Collins, 1968.

Kanable, Anna. *Raising Rabbits*. Emmaus, PA: Rodale Press, 1977.

Leach, Michael. *The Rabbit*. Aylesbury, England: Shire Natural History Series, 1980.

Naether, Carl A. *The Book of the Domestic Rabbit*. New York: David McKay, 1967.

Porter, Keith. *Discovering Rabbits and Hares*. New York: Bookwright Press, 1986.

Sheail, John. *Rabbits and Their History*. Newton Abbot, England: David & Charles, 1971.

BATS

Ackerman, Diane. "A Reporter at Large." *The New Yorker*, Feb. 29, 1988.

Allen, Glover Morrill. *Bats.* Cambridge, MA: Harvard University Press, 1939.

Barbour, R. W., and W. H. Davis. *Bats of America.* Lexington, KY: University of Kentucky Press, 1969.

Campbell, C. A. *Bats, Mosquitoes and Dollars.* Boston: The Stratford Co., 1925.

Couffer, Jack. *Bat Bomb: World War II's Other Secret Weapon.* Austin, Texas: University of Texas Press, 1992.

Fenton, M. Brock. *Just Bats.* Toronto: University of Toronto Press, 1983.

Fullard, James H. "Predator and Prey: Life and Death Struggles." *Bats*, Summer 1991.

Greenhall, A. M. "Use of Mist Nets and Strychnine for Vampire Control in Trinidad." *Journal of Mammology*, 44 (1963).

Griffin, Donald. *Listening in the Dark.* New Haven, CT: Yale University Press, 1958.

Harrison, Virginia. *The World of Bats.* Milwaukee, WI: Gareth Stevens Publishing, 1989.

Lauber, Patricia. *Bats: Wings in the Night.* New York: Random House, 1968.

Ludlow, G. W., and M. B. Fenton. "Control of Nursery Colony Population of Bats by Artificial Light." *Journal of Wildlife Management*, 35.

Novacek, Michael. "Navigators of the Night." *Natural History*, Oct. 1988.

Novick, A. and Nina Leen. *The World of Bats.* New York: Holt, Rinehart, 1970.

Pringle, Lawrence. *Batman: Exploring the World of Bats.* New York: Scribner's, 1991.

Racey, P. A., and D. M. Potts. "Relationship Between Stored Spermatazoa and the Uterine Epithelium in the Pipistrelle Bat." *Journal of Reproduction & Fertility*, 22, 1970.

Slaughter, Bob H., and Dan W. Walton, Eds. *About Bats: A Chiropteran Biology Symposium.* Dallas: Southern Methodist University Press, 1970.

Theroux, Alexander. "Twinkle, Twinkle, Little Bat . . . How We Wonder What He's At." *Reader's Digest*, Jan. 1984.

Tuttle, Merlin D. *America's Neighborhood Bats: Understanding and Learning to Live in Harmony With Them.* Austin, TX: University of Texas Press, 1988.

————. "Harmless, Highly Beneficial, Bats Still Get a Bum Rap." *Smithsonian*, Jan. 1984.

Yalden, D. W., and P. A. Morris. *The Lives of Bats.* New York: Quadrangle/New York Times Book Co., 1975.

SWANS

Ephron, Nora. *Heartburn.* New York: Knopf, 1983.

King, Deborah. *Swan*; *Story Told by Naomi Lewis.* New York: Lothrop, Lee & Shepard, 1985.

Paca, Lillian Grace. *The Royal Birds.* New York: St. Martin's Press, 1963.

Putnam, Alice. *The Whistling Swans.* New York: Julian Messner, 1981.

Schulberg, Budd. *Swan Watch.* New York: Delacorte Press, 1975.

Scott, Peter, and The Wildfowl Trust. *The Swans.* Boston: Houghton-Mifflin, 1972.

Index